Palgrave Studies in Victims and Victimology

Series Editors
Pamela Davies, Department of Social Sciences,
Northumbria University, Newcastle upon Tyne, UK
Tyrone Kirchengast, Law School, University of Sydney,
Sydney, NSW, Australia

In recent decades, a growing emphasis on meeting the needs and rights of victims of crime in criminal justice policy and practice has fuelled the development of research, theory, policy and practice outcomes stretching across the globe. This growth of interest in the victim of crime has seen victimology move from being a distinct subset of criminology in academia to a specialist area of study and research in its own right. *Palgrave Studies in Victims and Victimology* showcases the work of contemporary scholars of victimological research and publishes some of the highest-quality research in the field. The series reflects the range and depth of research and scholarship in this burgeoning area, combining contributions from both established scholars who have helped to shape the field and more recent entrants. It also reflects both the global nature of many of the issues surrounding justice for victims of crime and social harm and the international span of scholarship researching and writing about them.

Olumide Adisa · Emma Bond
Editors

Tackling Domestic Abuse and Sexual Violence

A Systems Approach

Editors
Olumide Adisa
University of Suffolk
Ipswich, UK

Emma Bond
University of Suffolk
Ipswich, UK

ISSN 2947-9355   ISSN 2947-9363   (electronic)
Palgrave Studies in Victims and Victimology
ISBN 978-3-031-58599-9   ISBN 978-3-031-58600-2   (eBook)
https://doi.org/10.1007/978-3-031-58600-2

Cover illustration: Floriana/Getty Images

This Palgrave Macmillan imprint is published by the registered company Springer Nature Switzerland AG
The registered company address is: Gewerbestrasse 11, 6330 Cham, Switzerland

If disposing of this product, please recycle the paper.

Foreword

Globally, we are challenged to design programmes or interventions to reduce domestic abuse & sexual violence (DASV) and mitigate its long-term impact within complex systems. These systems range from healthcare services, criminal justice, and to societal structures. Understanding and addressing the context of interventions is important, yet we need to move beyond context to a deeper understanding of how the interactions within a system can promote or act as obstacles to prevention and mitigation of DASV.

Explicit theoretical (and conceptual) frameworks enhance the quality of research and the design of interventions, also informing implementation and scaling up of successful programmes. Yet theoretical frameworks often have not directly informed interventions. In the past decade, conventional theories of change (with their linear assumptions) have become widespread. This edited volume by Adisa & Bond injects life into the theoretical and conceptualisation table in a new (and not-so-new) way by re-emphasising the need for a non-linear, interactive understanding of sustained systems change. As Adisa and Bond have highlighted in their "Introduction", they offer systemic understandings and emergent possibilities for future inquiry and reimaginings. The edited collection is an open invitation for a resurgence of understanding the role of a systems focus. Given that there are 10 different types of systems analysis (as documented by Michael C. Jackson), their wide-ranging collection focuses on critical systems thinking (CST) and its application to understanding and reducing DASV and its impact on survivors and society.

This edited collection comes at a crucial time for policy and practice for DASV in the UK and globally, with the advent of the Domestic Abuse Act in the UK and a growing commitment to reducing gender-based violence by international organisations and non-governmental organisations. This is a crucial time for the use of ideas in this collection to surface further some of the goals, contradictions, and tensions that underpin the systemic design of interventions for violence prevention and mitigation at every level. There is a need for wider prioritisation and integration of responses which call for theoretical thinking tools that do not shy away from the complex interactions between the different sectors and between different stakeholders. This collection gives us such an approach and perspective supported by case studies exemplifying this sort of complexity and addressing systemic improvement.

Academics researching domestic abuse and sexual violence (DASV) engage in explicit theory development, while others base their research on implicit theories. An example of the former is Marianne Hester's 3 planets model, which—explicitly rooted in Bourdieu's theory of *habitus*—articulates the disconnect between work with victims and perpetrators of DASV, child safeguarding, and child contact. An example of the latter is my own research, evaluating interventions for DASV survivors and people who use violence, with epistemological roots in the measurement of outcomes. Yet theory is everywhere, including in our measurement tools and assumptions in intervention development, which need to be surfaced and scrutinised in their complexity.

Built around retrospective case studies of the application of critical system thinking methods to DASV programmes, the editors have delivered more than a compelling compilation of examples. They have achieved something innovative and ambitious by working with some chapter authors who had developed and evaluated programmes without being aware of the CST perspective. In dialogue with the editors, the chapter authors were able to frame their work within that perspective. The editors did not impose or require this and took a more or less active role in specific chapter writing (co-authoring some). The CST characteristic of many of the chapters *emerged* from a kind of curatorial activity on the part of the editors. As you would expect, emergence is an important feature of complex systems.

The editors of this collection make a strong case for the added value of the explicit application of CST for driving change to what they term the DASV system. One of CST's principles is critical awareness, and the collection embodies this by paying homage to many aspects of critical system thinking that are already visible in DASV research. For instance, Adisa and Bond, towards the end of their chapter, point to the pioneering research and service development work of Liz Kelly and the late Ellen Pence, respectively. Yet, this is a landmark first book collection, applying CST across many sectors where DASV needs a systemic response, highlighting the potential of a system-wide analysis in various DASV settings. The chapter authors are an eclectic mix of academics, policymakers, practitioners, and service providers, ensuring the relevance of the book within and out with the academic world.

It is still unclear how much added value CST will ultimately deliver to DASV research and practice, but this book is a start in applying CST to our understanding of DASV, the development of DASV systemic interventions across sectors, and their robust evaluation, as we think beyond context into understandings of complexity. The book challenges assumptions, a core function of complex system theory, and is an important step towards its application to the real-world challenges of violence prevention.

Bristol, England, UK   Gene Feder OBE FMedSci

Preface

Like a butterfly emerging from its cocoon, *Tackling Domestic Abuse and Sexual Violence: A Systems Approach* emerged as an evolving idea, from a series of Domestic Abuse Research Network (DARNet) https://www.uos.ac.uk/our-research/research-institutes/institute-for-social-justice-and-crime/domestic-abuse-research-network-darnet/ conference webinar discussions, since its establishment in 2019.

Failing systems, and *systems failing* victims-survivors continued to permeate these conversations, further exacerbated by the Covid-19 pandemic crisis and cost—of—living crisis. Therefore, it became important to focus on the notion of 'systems' for this first edited collection.

As Editors, we both deeply care about tackling violence and abuse in all its forms, through transformational research, theorising, policy, and practice. This text aims to encourage a greater use of systems approach to optimise the interactions and relationships among individuals, groups, communities, as well as policy and national efforts concerned with tackling domestic abuse. Critical awareness, a commitment to improvement, and system alignment of shared goals and purpose, form the core of the text. All the authors identified actors and institutions within the system (and subsystems) they work in, and their case studies allowed these more expansive explorations to be undertaken, some of which have not been previously published. The contributing authors include practitioners, policymakers, and academics. Most of the chapters have engaged with retrospective case studies to newly engage with a systems approach to discover new thinking and applications, that may best suit the area of domestic abuse and sexual violence (DASV).

All the chapters showcase systems approach in varying ways to ignite new inquiries and conversations for grappling with greater levels of complexity of problems. The selection of case study examples underscores the relational importance of elements, interconnections in systems, bound up in a shared purpose of tackling DASV through systems change. Part of the aspiration of this book is to help those interested in learning about selected critical systems approaches in uncovering interactions and boundary judgements and to offer an accessible foundational engagement to the systems approach field. Additionally, this text aims to bridge the highly technical jargon field of systems theory to the pragmatic concerns of DASV, which increasing complexity necessitates a more than 'whole-of-the-system' perspective to tackle the wicked problem of DASV.

Suffolk, UK   Olumide Adisa, Ph.D.
                                                              Emma Bond, Ph.D.

Acknowledgements

Anything worthwhile takes time to build. This edited collection, which pragmatically explores a systems approach, has benefitted from the open-mindedness and generosity of many people. This volume provides an exciting and unique opportunity to purposefully experiment and think with those at the forefront of their subject and practice. We sincerely thank these brilliant authors who accepted our invitation to contribute to this field-building venture. Each of their unique perspectives and insights have enriched this work immensely. We also extend our gratitude to the anonymous peer reviewers, whose critical comments have added depth and greatly improved the work.

Special thanks to Gene Feder for writing an excellent Foreword to draw out insightful messages about this edited collection.

On a personal note, Olumide would like to thank her close family and friends, especially Zion, who was birthed during the editing of this book and who provided much-needed inspiration when she most needed it. She would especially like to thank everyone who encouraged her as she continues to surface the value of complex systems thinking in bringing about sustained change in ending violence and abuse. Many people she greatly admires shared their knowledge, contacts, and experience at various points, including in everyday spontaneous conversations: Thanks especially to Meena Kumari, Ruth Weir, Laurelle Brown, Suzanne Jacob, Jo Todd CBE, Kyla Kirkpatrick, Roxanne Khan, Glenn Robinson, Nicole Jacobs, Beryl Foster, Sally McManus, Gerald Midgley, Claire Waxman OBE, Chris Bonnell, Hiroki Sayama, Nicola Sharp-Jeffs, Sarah Richards, and Amanda McCormick (in no particular order).

She is grateful to Holly Smith and colleagues at the Brotherton Research Centre at the University of Leeds, who were so helpful and welcoming as she (unsuccessfully) explored systems thinking in the WAFE Archive. She is also thankful to her colleagues at the University of Suffolk and on the VISION Consortium at City University of London, who continue to engage with her ideas on complex systems change.

Olumide would also like to thank Emma for her generous scholarship, friendship, and championing of this edited collection.

Finally, our sincere thanks to everyone at Palgrave Macmillan, who were a delight to work with. We especially want to thank Josie Taylor, an engaged editor who was supportive throughout the process, Hemapriya Eswanth and Jayalakshmi Raju, who made the production process go so smoothly.

Contents

Notes on Contributors

Katherine Allen is a Senior Research Fellow in the Institute for Social Justice and Crime at the University of Suffolk. She has cross-disciplinary research experience in social policy, philosophy, and literature, with strong research interests in sexual/gender-based violence and the evolution of feminist ending violence movements, feminist and social epistemology, and philosophy of literature, mind and the emotions.

Olumide Adisa is Senior Research Fellow at the University of Suffolk and Complex Systems Theory Lead/Co-Investigator on the VISION Consortium at City University, London, UK. She founded the Domestic Abuse Research Network (DARNet). As an engaged academic in the sector, she brings an enormous breadth and depth of knowledge and experience on domestic abuse, improving services and commissioning for all victims/survivors, and developing complex systems change approaches for violence prevention and mitigation.

Richard Baldwin is Head of Community Safety with over 25 years of experience working within a range of services for local government. Richard is a keen advocate for community-centred responses to 'wicked' community safety priorities such as domestic abuse and has been instrumental in developing initiatives such as domestic abuse champions to support a response grounded in communities. Richard also has a Master's degree in public Sector Leadership and Management.

Emma Bond is Pro-Vice Chancellor Research, and Professor of Socio-Technical Research at the University of Suffolk, UK. Emma has extensive research experience focusing on online risk and vulnerable groups, image-based abuse (sexting and revenge pornography), online harassment, domestic abuse, and sexual abuse, and she is internationally renowned for her work on online safeguarding.

Joana Ferreira is a Lecturer in Criminology at the University of Bath. Her research interests revolve mainly around violence against women, intimate partner abuse, and social justice. She has an M.Phil. in Criminological Research and a Ph.D. in Criminology, with a comparative study on Intimate Partner Violence Victims' Perceptions and Experiences of Criminal Justice Interventions in England and Portugal. She is also a trained Victim Support Officer.

Margaret Hill is a Domestic Services Manager. She has worked with survivors and victims of domestic abuse within the charity sector for over 20 years, delivering and developing frontline services.

Meena Kumari is a safeguarding expert and the Founder/Director of H.O.P.E Training & Consultancy. As a response to the COVID-19 pandemic, she developed and led national Domestic Abuse calls within racially minoritised communities. She has worked in frontline services since 2005 with victims, perpetrators and children/young people. She is currently leading a leadership programme for staffing working within the ending violence against women and girls sector.

Carolyn Leader is a Lecturer in Early Childhood Studies at the University of Suffolk. In 2015, Carolyn qualified with an Advanced Diploma in Psychotherapeutic Counselling. Carolyn holds a 1st class B.A. Hons in Early Childhood Studies. Carolyn holds a Master's in Sociology from Essex and was awarded a distinction in her thesis, and Master's degree overall. Carolyn's Masters' thesis focused on gender performances and was entitled 'Swipe it Right: An exploration into finding Tinder Charming'. She researches the role of technology in domestic abuse.

Mark Manning is a Visiting Senior Fellow in Policing Justice and Crime at the University of Suffolk within the Institute of Social Justice and Crime. He spent much of his working life as a serving police officer entering Higher Education upon retirement, teaching Criminology whilst researching for his Ph.D. His research interests are closely related to policing and criminal justice.

Lisa Pack is a Domestic Abuse Project Co-ordinator. For the last 19 years, she has worked for a specialist domestic abuse agency, providing support to service users and co-ordinating an outreach team. She was part of a multi-agency partnership team providing advocacy and holistic support to migrant victims of domestic abuse identifying as NRTPF.

Andy Phippen is a Professor of Online Harms at Bournemouth University. He has specialised in the use of ICTs in social and ethical contexts and the intersection with legislation for over 20 years, carrying out a large amount of grassroots research around internet safety and contemporary issues such as sexting, surveillance tech, and digital well-being.

Emily Setty is a Senior Lecturer in Criminology at the University of Surrey. She conducts research with young people about their experiences of sex and relationships, including nude image sharing, pornography, and consent, among other topics. She works with national and frontline practitioners and policymakers to develop interventions that address young people's issues and challenges.

Katie Tyrrell is a Research Fellow at the University of Suffolk, and Ph.D. student studying technology-facilitated intimacy in Higher Education. Since joining the university, Katie has worked alongside local, national, and international organisations to investigate the impact of interventions upon the welfare and well-being of people across the lifespan using creative and mixed methods approaches.

List of Figures

List of Tables

Introduction

Olumide Adisa and Emma Bond

There are no separate systems. The world is a continuum. Where to draw
a boundary around a system depends on the purpose of the discussion.
—Donella (Dana) Meadows (2008)[1]

There is an African proverb which goes thus, *'A tree on a hill in the
savannah is a meeting place for birds'*, suggesting that everything in (social,
economic, and political) systems is connected in interdependent ways.
Taking action in one component (e.g. felling the tree or removing the

---

[1] Quote from Thinking in Systems: A Primer by Donella Meadows. Her text which was
completed following her death arguably paved the way in making systems thinking more
approachable and to inspire new systems thinking tools for a better future.

O. Adisa (✉) · E. Bond
University of Suffolk, Ipswich, UK
e-mail: o.adisa@uos.ac.uk

E. Bond
e-mail: e.bond@uos.ac.uk

© The Author(s), under exclusive license to Springer Nature
Switzerland AG 2024
O. Adisa and E. Bond (eds.), *Tackling Domestic Abuse and Sexual Violence*, Palgrave
Studies in Victims and Victimology, https://doi.org/10.1007/978-3-031-58600-2_1

birds) affects other components of the ecosystem. Both this proverb and the quote above underscore why a preoccupation with systems (as a *raison d'etre* in this text) is a useful endeavour in the area of tackling violence and abuse. If one is to accept that everything is interconnected and that the whole is greater than the sum of its parts, then thinking systemically matters. The notion of 'systems' in its interconnectedness (whether as theory, metaphors or concepts) is a way of understanding and knowing in its own right—at least in ontological and epistemic terms.

For some who have been in the complex arena of tackling domestic abuse and sexual violence (DASV) for a long time, taking a systems view is one of an intuitive and pragmatic necessity, to grapple with complexity and change which does not adhere to linear cause and effect understandings. One could then ask, *how might systems change be best understood in tackling DASV systems, in the face of complexity (multiple complex needs, volatility, crises, unpredictability, and so on)?* While to others, the sense of systems thinking and systems approaches, even in its applied sense, to concerns in the violence and abuse sphere, may bring with it a certain amount of scholarly scepticism, and in one extreme case, may foster a friendly eruption of bemusement. Nonetheless, the modest concern of this text is with respect to the *usefulness* of a systems approach. Concerning DASV, it proposes systems approaches as a more expansive and encompassing response for understanding, re(aligning), and (re)thinking systemic interventions in a context of complexity. In the first part of the volume, we focus on multi-agency and community-based responses and applications. The second part of the volume offers tools and conceptual tools for engendering systems thinking. The third and final part of the volume highlights other institutional applications and applications of systems approaches.

Systems thinking as a field of study is not new, but the scholarly application of systems approaches and concepts to DASV issues across various systems in a collection is arguably an original project. Systems thinking is an umbrella term for a variety of methods, tools, and ideas, that has had over three decades of development by scholars across disciplines, from psychology (Stanton and Welsh, 2012) to operational research, public health (Carey et al., 2015; Orr et al., 2023), and the management sciences (Jackson, 2019) to name a few. Systems thinking and its applications are vast, with several theories, definitions, and perspectives on what systems thinking means. As others have noted, for a field of study that is aimed at promoting an understanding of systems to solve complex problems, it has become complex in itself—a system within a system, and of nested and unnested subsystems (Meadows, 2008; Williams & Imam, 2007), alongside many abundant metaphors and analogies to describe real-world systems and problems. Contemporary systems thinkers, Derek and Laura Cabrera's accessible definition is a useful springboard for introducing this book's direction:

> *Systems thinking is the field of study that attempts to understand how to think better about real-world systems and the real-world problems that we face.*
> —Cabrera and Cabrera (2015)

At its core, the emergence of systems thinking began as an alternative for mitigating the limits of reductionism and the scientific method, and to account for multiple perspectives on a complex issue which may be often challenging to reconcile (Midgley, 2001). One advantage of thinking and seeing everything in 'systems' terms is that we can better articulate goals and take action in relation to interrelationships and interconnections, rather than in silos or isolated components. A systems view brings to sharp focus the need for creating supportive contexts for sustainable systemic change.

Systems thinking is multi-perspective, improvement-driven, and methodologically pluralist. This important approach and/or worldview to exploring complex real-problems through systems thinking has been described as 'systemism'. According to Poe Yu-se Wan, systemism is an attempt to come to grips with the complexity of a phenomena and is a worldview that investigates all things as a system or subsystem, which is made of elements and components (Wan, 2013). All systems (natural or human) typically have a function or purpose (Meadows, 2008, p. 15).

The Foremost contemporary systems thinker Michael C. Jackson documented ten individual systems approaches[2] which are dominant in

---

[2] These are: (1) operational research, systems analysis, systems engineering (also known as hard systems thinking), (2) the vanguard method, (3) systems dynamics, (4) socio-technical

the transdisciplinary systems thinking literature. It is impossible to do justice to the synthesis of the vast field of systems thinking here, and readers are directed to the comprehensive volume by Jackson (2019) for a thorough discussion.

Jackson further noted that there is a risk of 'pigeon-holing' in choosing a selective focus to begin one's journey of systems thinking, and in applying to practice, but that we must begin somewhere (Jackson, 2019, p. xxvi). We agree, also.

And so, because in this book, we share an affinity with systems thinking principles that embrace a *critical awareness* view, systemic improvement, and pluralist interdisciplinary leanings, we consider the field of critical systems thinking (CST) to be the most suitable approach to pitch our tent in an inspirational attempt at integrating systems thinking to DASV domains. Although a couple of the technology-oriented chapters also explore a socio-technical systems approach, critical systems thinking is predominantly the area that we have engaged with the most in this text due to this approach's pragmatic suitability for the DASV sphere, and we go into more detail later in this introductory chapter, and as described throughout the chapters of this text.

CST is a variant of systems thinking developed by Gerald Midgley and his colleagues at the University of Hull in the 1990s. According to Midgley (cited in Flood and Romm, 1997, p. 11), the three 'commitments' of CST are: critical awareness (sweeping in of diverse perspectives), emancipation (an appreciation for improvement), and methodological pluralism (an appreciation of different unconventional methods). CST sees the whole system as fully unknowable but uses these three principles to encourage system-oriented responsiveness and expansionist thinking for bringing about long-term change through DASV interventions. Concerning violence against women and girls, and to underscore CST's suitability to this wicked problem of violence and abuse, to our knowledge, international development evaluators, Ellen Lewis and Anne Stephens, have attempted to apply Midgley's ideas to the

---

systems thinking, (5) organisational cybernetics and the viable systems model, (6) strategic assumption, surfacing and testing, (7) interactive planning, (8) Soft systems methodology, (9) Team syntegrity, and (10) Critical systems thinking and heuristics.

sustainable development goals agenda, by taking a feminist and critical systems approach to programme and policy evaluation (UN, 2018).

The next section introduces the reader to the key assumptions of systems thinking and ideas deployed in this book. We recognise that 'thinking in systems', and systems approaches applications are relatively new concepts for tackling complex phenomena like DASV, and so we have not assumed specialist knowledge on systems theory and approaches, and as Editors (and co-authors) we have tried to make this text accessible to non-specialist readers.

The Key Ideas Shaping This Book

Human Systems, and DASV as a Wicked Problem

Human systems are characterised by increasing complexity which make problems challenging to solve. In his last book, 'Human Systems are Different' systems scientist Geoffery Vickers (1894–1982) convincingly argued for an appreciation of human systems as complex systems that are very different to, say tackling engineering problems (Vickers, 1983). Human systems when viewed through a 'wicked problem' lens are socially constructed, but wicked problems, (as coined by Horst Rittel and Melvin Webber) are impossible to resolve (Rittel and Webber, 1973).

The framing of domestic abuse and sexual violence as a wicked problem foregrounds the book's value and contribution clearly and succinctly. There is often a sense that the tackling DASV sphere is in a hopeless situation due to the numerous interventions and dualistic arguments on what is the best approach to take to tackling DASV (for example, should one focus on: victims/perpetrators, prevention/provision, criminalisation/rehabilitation, and so on). Without discounting the useful contributions of those whose tireless work and endeavours may fall solely within these single/binary components or categories, this text is best viewed as a hopeful reaction that our efforts need to be directed towards relational and collective systems approaches, which emphasise a greater sense of interconnectedness and interdependencies in systems.

No debate is necessary about how tackling wicked problems such as domestic abuse and sexual violence is primarily about saving and transforming lives. This volume argues that for this to occur, we need to think more in systems, and develop systemic interventions based on this thinking. The need for transformative systems change in our society to combat the devastating human and societal costs caused by DASV which does not seem to be abating, has never been greater. With so much at stake with respect to the devastating costs of violence and abuse, there is a strong argument for how systems might be recalibrated and/or optimised to tackle root crises in a context of complexity and multiplied crises. This text sees innovative 'theoretical' approaches like critical systems thinking in DASV concerns as a potential for transforming systems. Here, in this book, for instance, we demonstrate through various retrospective case studies how critical systems thinking, and approaches can be applied in different settings and systems—individual and groups (Chapters 3, 6), community (Chapters 3, 4), institutional (schools, universities, policing) (Chapters 7, 8, and 9).

There is no universal definition of systems, but the accessible definition below by Meadows suffices to introduce the main concept guiding this book.

> "A system is more than the sum of its parts" (Meadows, 2008; p.12)… a system typically comprises of "three kinds of things: elements, interconnections, and a function or purpose". (p. 11)

Meadows provides a useful analogy in thinking about systems and subsystems as thus, 'an animal is a system. A tree is a system, and a forest is a larger system that encompasses subsystems of trees and animals' (Ibid). Naming something gives validity to the thing and helps in understanding the roots and how the shifts are taking place in this area of work. In systems theory parlance, by having this common language of viewing something as systemic, scholars can overcome the 'limitations of their fragmentary disciplines' (Midgley, 2001, p. 34). Of course, it is not always necessary to ground systems terminology and concepts in its etymology to justify its value, but given that the etymology exists, it provides an opportunity to further define what we mean by a 'system'.

Originating first within the field of sciences, we find the early origin of systems defined in relation to life sciences ecosystems, 'organised whole, and sum of vital processes in an organism'. In relation to technology/cybernetics, it has been defined as far back as the 1960s in relation to 'a group of related programs'. A system can be characterised or perceived as a set of relationships in which the elements when taken together form a whole. The whole itself may be part of wider system (s) with their own set of elements that are linked to other systems. Already this suggests that regardless of how you look at the world, one cannot get away from encountering a system and systems to make sense of the world and to improve one's world. The concept of 'system' itself can be used for problem-solving issues that relate to human situations—these are often 'messy' issues that are often complex and not easily resolved, like wicked problems.

Earlier, we have framed DASV as a wicked problem occurring in human systems, so can this problem be solved? Emerita Professor on violence extremism, Lynn Davies argues that wicked problems 'cannot be solved at all, that is impossible—all that is possible is that the problem space is loosened', and to allow for more innovative approaches to emerge (Davies, 2016, p. 32). Still, we must be cautious about what is possible for 'loosening the problem space' on DASV through a systems thinking lens, and so, this text is supported by retrospective case studies in which the authors apply selected aspects of CST, and this book is a first attempt at embarking on such an enterprise.

Ecosystem Thinking

In two of the chapters (Chapters 3 and 8), the well-established ecological framework has been used to Bronfenbrenner's (1979) Ecology of Human Development to depict and surface components, ecosystems thinking, and conducive environments. The DASV landscape is complex and can be understood as a complex system with inter-related and interconnections made up of actors (survivors, commissioners, services, communities, etc.), aligned to a purpose. In Chapter 3, Adisa collaborates with Ferreira, Hill, and Pack, to apply the Bronfenbrenner's (1979) ecological model further to depict understandings of a migrant survivor's inter-relationship with the ecosystem diagrammatically against backdrop of 'interconnecting social, political and economic conditions' (Kelly, 2016). Additionally, Bond joins Tyrrell, and Phippen in Chapter 8, and they artfully marshall this ecological framework to make the case that the most effective context for human development, relies on not just looking at the individual, but the environment as well.

Theory of Boundary Critique

To further sharpen the critical edge of this book, we draw on critical systems heuristics, which has emerged from Werner Ulrich's theory of boundary critique. The theory of boundary critique is an open approach for surfacing boundary judgements (Ulrich, 1996, 2005) and builds on Churchman's notion of improvement through stakeholder involvement. The idea of improvement is based on the early work of C. West Churchman in the late 1960s to 1970s. Churchman was committed to the notion of the improvement and first put forward the thesis on the importance of sweeping in information for improvement. Churchman's main contribution was in expanding the thinking around boundaries in relation to systems. Churchman's understanding of a system assumes that relevant knowledge does not come from just one group. In other words, a key feature is the role of stakeholders in transcending disciplinary boundaries, as against deferring to one dominant perspective. Churchman further argues that the lack of comprehensiveness from having different diverse perspectives can be overcome by sweeping in more information to generate insights about a situation; and that how much sweeping in can occur to define and frame a system depends on boundary judgements in place (Churchman, 1970).

This idea of sweeping in information is important in critical systems thinking, but humans tend to make boundary judgements (based on values, norms, and facts), and this use of system boundary judgements can influence not only the type of system design for tackling DASV but also bring in more complexity, which further makes it challenging to surface assumptions and for sense-making on how to bring about systems change or to improve the system. A good example is in the ways that some organisations or different helping systems (for example, mental health services, employment support services) may not consider domestic abuse to be their core business. In this book, the case studies on Rape Crisis Centres (Chapter 6), and the criminal justice system (Chapter 9) provide a rich discussion on the implications of boundary judgements.

Ulrich contends that without understanding boundaries and boundaries categories, thinking about systems can lead to the risk of continual expansion and a loss of meaning, however he further argues that boundary judgements are not absolute. Boundary judgements and value judgements then are interlinked and as such we need boundary critique to further understand how system boundaries have been defined, and by whom. Boundary lines tell us where something begins and ends. However, it can also reveal what is included and what is excluded within in. Midgley's CST is coupled with Ulrich's CSH due to the former's contributions to the boundary critique, specifically in adding to the critique, a question about where moral responsibility for improvement lies for individuals and communities (Midgley, 2001, p. 149). It is in this examination of philosophical assumptions that sets out Midgley's contribution to the development of Ulrich's theory of boundary critique. Boundaries can be used to depict complexity but can also generate complexity as a result of these boundary decision-making issues. But boundaries can also help to engender understandings of systems, and as such Midgley argues that the boundary concept must be the core of systems thinking (Midgley, 2001).

Systems Change Through *Systemic* Interventions

Here in this book, we demonstrate that there are a multitude of complex interconnected events and elements at play in any systemic intervention or system, which warrant a focus on complex systems change. In this text, we define a systemic intervention as one designed to generate sustainable, and transformational outcomes for stakeholders and beneficiaries in complex systems (Adisa et al., 2023). Systems change approaches are increasingly used by those aiming to develop effective responses to complex social issues, which have defied 'clean, simple' solutions based on traditional linear theories of change (Imam et al., 2007, p. 7).

A systemic intervention by design is more amenable to bringing about systems change and for evaluating these systems change. For example, Adisa (2023)'s theory-based systems change framework[3] which has been adapted prospectively to a systemic intervention on those working with harmful behaviours has been reproduced here to depict the elements of the framework, used to depict the interacting components of how systems change happens, and represents a CST evaluation in the DASV sphere. (See Appendix Table 1, for a glossary of these terms.)

Some of these terms and assumptions provided a common language to also further explore and theme the insights with collaborators of this text, and to reveal the reality of the various actors and relationships that influence systems across our retrospective case study examples (Fig. 1).

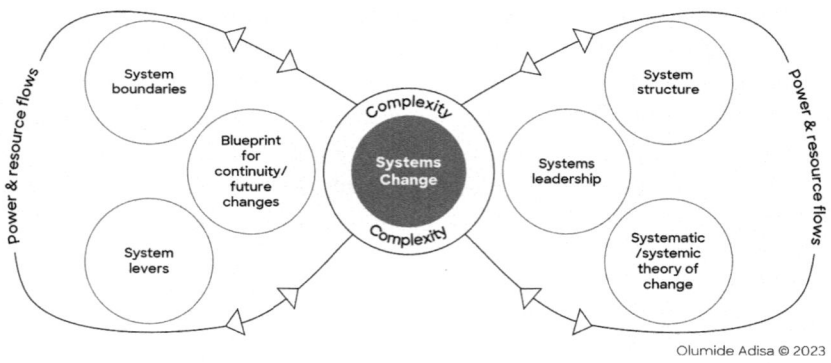

Olumide Adisa © 2023

Fig. 1   A suggested theory-based systems framework for action and evaluation

---

[3] The assumptions guiding this proposed framework are as follows: Change is constrained by the systems we live within; no social change happens in a vacuum. A will not be optimised (project outcomes) if B (the 'whole' system) is not aligned to the goals to be achieved; local systems may differ/or not from national systems; systems are nested or un-nested within subsystems and require multiple systems to be described as such. When actions are fragmentary, it leads to poorer outcomes for victims and survivors. Systems can be hidden and/or visible in its form and function; and that there is no getting away from complexity. Complex systems change provides a more encompassing and flexible approach to systems change through grappling with complexity.

Theoretically, and as mentioned earlier, it is not possible to fully know a system, because the whole is always greater than the sum of its parts (Meadows, 2008) as highlighted earlier. Additionally, not all system elements or subsystems are visible, and in these cases, 'below the surface' systems (Foster-Fishman & Behrens, 2007, p. 204) are just as important as the above the surface systems to bring about systems change. So how does one change a system that is understandable but not fully knowable? One approach may be to draw on complex systems dynamics concepts to further grip complexity across time–space boundaries. Projects (and organisations) operate within complexity and the Covid-19 crisis, Brexit, and the cost-of-living impacts have brought this into sharp focus and demand new tools for making sense of this complexity in changing the structure and behaviour of systems. For an introductory text on systems thinking for DASV, aimed at an informed public (beyond academia), engagement with the full menu of complex systems concepts was outside the scope of the book. However, in this book, we recognise that complexity in systems matters, and deserves a dedicated focus, and this theoretical and integration work has already begun elsewhere through the involvement of one of the Editors (Adisa) in the VISION Consortium at the Violence and Society Centre at City University of London.

We began by saying that we want this book to be as useful as possible to many people. And we were lucky that during the writing of this book, we had people ask how one may begin to identify relevant systems thinking components (including mapping) for systems change.

We have reproduced Adisa's framework here as a helpful suggestion for the applicability of issues for systems thinking in practical terms—at the very least to engender new conversations. The complexity-aware systems change framework below maps to some of the case study settings. Our intention is not to suggest a universalising approach (this defeats the point of critical systems thinking), nonetheless we recognise that people will have to start somewhere, and being able to identify some systems change components (already tested in practice) further pragmatises systems thinking.

As a result, in all the chapters, the authors may use terms like systems change, transformation, levers of change, boundaries, and so on. Some of the case studies give primary attention to identifying and describing activities that lend themselves to uncovering the characteristics of systems and the interconnected elements that work well together to achieve a shared purpose of systems change, as an example. Others take a more theoretical approach, which certainly lends a fascinating contribution to the volume nonetheless.

What Can Systems Thinking Approaches Add to the DASV Sphere

As earlier mentioned, we problematise DASV as a 'wicked problem', and position critical systems thinking within the domestic abuse and sexual violence sphere as a useful conceptual tool in improving our understanding of wicked 'systemic' problems.

In this book, we demonstrate the importance of approaching some of the system-related issues of DASV in a systemic rather than through a component-by-component or piecemeal fashion. One good example is the mapping of the Violence Against Women and Girls (VAWG) funding ecosystem previously undertaken elsewhere by the Editors and others (Adisa et al, 2020). This systems approach is even more important in relation to rethinking and redesigning complex funding systems for DASV[4] (government, private donors, charitable trusts), and how this funding system might strategically mobilise and pool funds together to bring about sustainable systems change.

The terrain of tackling domestic abuse and sexual violence is shifting in complex ways that necessitate a rethinking of our systems. Thinking about policing as the sole response to domestic abuse is not a viable option. At the time of writing this book, there have been more media reports of high-profile cases of police-perpetrated domestic abuse and serious sexual offences. The proliferation and severity of these cases and the impacts on trust in policing are at a disaster level. These police officers should rightly be judged through the lens of the law. However,

---

[4] There are different systems involved in the preventing of violence and abuse (relating to intimate relationships), as well as provision of services, which brings in complexity into the system as a 'whole' and influences the degree to which systems change can be achieved.

the scale at which the cases are happening and organisational failures in investigating the cases and using intelligence when victims came forward is reminiscent of the failures of the social work system in preventing child abuse-related deaths in the early 2000s.

In the social work sphere, Eileen Munro (Munro Review of Child Protection) utilised a systemic approach to uncover the complexities and to make sense of what went wrong. Munro drew parallels between child protection and natural disasters—and that natural disasters are rarely found to occur due to the mistake of one individual but because of a system which has been functioning with a 'chronic pattern of small errors or omissions...' which then led to the tragic outcomes. Munro saw the issue as a problem of the system and advocated for the examination of the system rather than focusing solely on any one professional's mistakes (Munro, 2005, p. 533).

An example of a charity-led systems change approach to improve policing practice and bring greater consistency in knowledge and confidence of police officers responding to domestic abuse, and coercive and controlling behaviour incidents is Safelives' Domestic Abuse (DA) Matters training for police officers, which was conceived in 2014 and written with the College of Policing. By training and championing professionals across the UK to spot the early signs of domestic abuse and understand the tactics used by those using harmful behaviours, they aim to stop domestic abuse. At the core of the training programme, it aims to change and challenge attitudes, police culture and behaviours in responding to DA. Using data from police forces that have undergone DA matters training, a recent study found that force-wide training led to a 41% increase in arrests for controlling and coercive behaviour, although the researchers also found that the numbers of CCB arrests were 'miniscule' in relation to DA arrests (Brennan et al., 2021). The self-evaluation undertaken between 2017 and 2018 used feedback forms completed by 3,657 Domestic Abuse First Responders and by 361 Domestic Abuse Matters Champions and anecdotal evidence found that the training led to 'a change in attitude and thinking around domestic abuse' which then led to improvements in arrest rates and the overall response to those affected by domestic abuse (Safelives, 2018).

However, creating small incidental change in targeted systems in highly bureaucratic human service systems, such as the police, is noteworthy but has its limitations. While the police play a vital role in the response to domestic abuse, there are other important organisations operating inside and outside the criminal justice system (e.g. statutory health agencies, educational institutions) who can also influence the outcomes experienced by victims and survivors. Chapter 9 (Mark Manning) further elaborates on these complexities of the criminal justice system as a 'whole' reference system with boundary decision-making implications, and the implications of the rights of victim-survivors through a lens of alignment/misalignment of values, and political and socio-cultural thought.

Systems change efforts that focus solely on one aspect of the picture tend to have the tendency to limit our understanding of the complex systems change that is needed to influence the overall response to victims and survivors but also to 'stop' domestic abuse.

Linked to this issue of incidental change, is that of episodic systems change (Foster-Fishman et al., 2007) which tend to be driven by short-term funding to organisations. This has been identified as a dysfunctionality and blockage in the VAWG funding ecosystem (Adisa et al., 2020) and may even have ramifications for systems leadership and episodic allyship (as explored in the chapter by Kumari and Adisa). In 2017, the UN classified systems thinking as one of the four ways of working that are important for international leadership and practice (see the UN System Leadership Framework[5]), and in this chapter an example of systems leadership in the DASV sphere is explored in the context of equity-oriented systems change.

Through our vast evaluation work on DASV, we also noted the dominant use of programme-focused approaches (e.g. conventional linear theory of change and service data before and after the intervention) rather than critical systems thinking intervention frameworks of evaluating the complex evidence. In simpler terms, we become heavily focused on *how the project works* but not necessarily about how people *think* they

---

[5] UN (2017). United Nations System Leadership Framework. CEB UN System Chief Executives Board for Coordination.

work within a system or where systems change efforts are misaligned due to a preoccupation or unhelpful obsession with tinkering with parts of the system.

One unintended consequence of this programmatic focus rather than a systems focus is that it leads to 'fuzzy' understandings of meaningful change that shifts systems. The hamster in a wheel metaphor best explains the futility of not tackling the issue of DASV through a systems view. Interventions continue to be developed to tinker with the parts rather than the 'whole' (it is helpful to assume that the system is structured and nested in this way, but unnested systems are also possible, debunking the idea of 'whole and sum of parts').

Theory of change (ToCs) approaches primarily focus on understanding how project elements (inputs, activities) have led to the outcomes achieved to demonstrate impact are useful in linking activities to outcomes in a linear fashion, however as an approach it is not effective in grappling with complexity within a system, which then limits our understanding of the full spectrum of actors, interactions and levers of change involved in the change process across multiple complex systems. At the time of writing, while there are now a handful of complexity-aware ToCs being used in the evaluation field and policy planning (see, e.g., the Defra Theory of Change Tool[6]), to encourage expansionist thinking and to identify complexities in interventions and policies, this is yet to be applied specifically to the DASV sphere.

In Search of Feminist System Thinkers in the DASV Academic Sphere

All knowledge is subject to the caprices of continuity and change and insights about the past are useful in understanding the present and future. In the systems literature, dominant masculinised lens, paradigms, and theories have greatly shaped systems theory and by extension the systems thinking field which draws from those theories in the complexity science field (see Castellani and Hafferty [2009] for a useful map of most

---

[6] Defra (2021). Defra Theory of Change Toolkit - SD1421. Department of Environment, Food and Rural Affairs.

of the field developments and founders), and so we started to ask, as one does with these things, where are all the women founders linked to the DASV sphere?

At the beginning of 2023, one of the Editors (Adisa) made a verbal call-out through various friends of DARNet and on Twitter/X to ask if there were older feminists (who were part of the early feminist movement building for tackling DASV), who were willing to talk about systems change, and systems thinking at the time. Adisa was able to speak to three inspiring women through this process. Time constraints did not permit a more robust expression of interest, but this is a matter for future research directions.

Adisa also visited the WAFE Archive[7] in September 2023 over the course of two days to explore early systems thinking historically. Recognising that campaigning, advocacy, and provision of accommodation were key concerns for mainstream feminists at the time, it is important to keep in mind that the challenges of the time (1970s–1980s) intersected with the pressure issues of surfacing domestic abuse issues in policy and political agendas; additionally that this brief study visit was a partial rapid deep dive into the archive that is still being catalogued. Interestingly, despite these (non)discoveries of mentions about systems, the process of discovery in the engagement with the Archive itself offered up new questions and avenues for a systems thinking (re)reading of two well-known feminists' writings, Liz Kelly, (SV) and Ellen Pence (1948–2012) (DA), in the DASV sphere.

We offer up these two examples here briefly due to space limitations. This is certainly not an exhaustive review. The aim here is to begin to potentially uncover a feminised systems thinking already formulated in relation to DASV—even it has been given a different name.

Liz Kelly (Continuum of Violence, 1980s)

Kelly (1988) contends that violence encompasses 'a continuous series of *elements* or events that pass into one another and cannot be readily

---

[7] Women's Aid Federation of England and Wales Archive.

distinguished' yet these different elements 'have a basic common character' (1988, p. 76). The use of certain terms in this definition is similar to systems thinking language, for example, the use of the word 'continuous' as used here can relate to the notion of feedback loops and circular causality, suggesting that violence follows a nonlinear representation. As Kelly argues in her first publication on the concept, Continuum of Sexual Violence:

> The concept should not be seen, therefore, as a linear straight line connecting the different events or experiences. There are a number of dimensions which affect the meaning for, and impact on, women of experiences of sexual violence, at the time they happened, and later in time. (Kelly, 1987, p. 48)

In anticipation of dualistic and reductionist debates on 'seriousness' in the interpretation of sexual violence, she further states that 'all forms of sexual violence are serious', (Ibid., p. 49), suggesting that the survivors' journeys are not reducible to one single story of victimisation on one end, and survival on the other. Additionally, the 'basic common character' alluded to in Kelly's continuum (p. 76) enables the theorisation of more expansive explanations beyond dominant binaristic characterisations of female victim/male perpetrator in understanding women's experiences of abuse (Boyle, 2019). The focus on understanding women's experiences of abuse as occurring in a continuum entails a structure that encompasses, the continuousness of the interconnections of the individual, institutional, and structural domains.

'Continuum thinking' (as coined by Karen Boyle) then could be re-read also as a form of systems thinking due to its emphasis on interconnections and interdependencies across time and space, but which are distinguishable from each other. Boyle suggests the need for pluralised forms of the term continuum ('continuums') to further signify 'differing sets of contexts and connections' (Boyle, 2019, p. 21) and a potential expansive notion of complexity theoretically.

Ellen Pence (Systems Change, 1990s)

Through recollections of two of the women who shared their views, feminists from the UK who attended the Change Conference in the United States met Ellen Pence (1948–2012),[8] and heard Pence train and teach on systems change, had an encounter which inspired a few UK-based feminist to return with those ideas to improve the criminal justice system. This led to the creation of the Coordinated Community Response (CCR) model in England and Wales[9] (also see Chapter 2), which the charity Standing Together Against Domestic Abuse (STADA/ST) has been pioneering and developing over the years. As one of the early founders of ST (formerly STADA) shares[10]:

> coordinated community responses are not meeting places to share information but it ought to be a group of people who analyse the system together, identify gaps and close them.

The first part of the statement shares an affinity to Lynn Davies' idea of the 'loosening of problem space' earlier mentioned, and the value of systems thinking lies in its collaborative endeavour to analyse and bring together systems in achieving this loosening. Pence calls this collaborative endeavour as systems advocacy. As she wrote:

> Making changes in procedures or policies in this network is complicated by the multiple sites of decision making. There is of course the formal, recognized division of tasks and power as well as the informal and often

---

[8] Ellen Pence was the cofounder of Domestic Abuse Intervention Programs, which originated in Duluth, Minnesota in the United Sates. She was instrumental in the 'replicating and expanding of the Duluth model, through its Coordinated Community Response' which brings agencies together to end DA (Domestic Abuse Intervention Programmes, n.d.) and her later work through Praxis International.

[9] "A CCR brings services together to ensure local systems truly keep survivors safe, hold abusers to account and prevent domestic abuse…it enables a whole system response to a whole person. It shifts responsibility for safety away from individual survivors to the community and services existing to support them" (*Source* STADA. [n.d.]. What is CCR. Available at: https://www.standingtogether.org.uk/what-is-ccr).

[10] These are the views of an individual and should not be taken as the charity's official position.

more contested terrain of policy making. Systems advocacy requires advocates to promote changes that take into account the multiple agendas of intervening agencies while maintaining their own priority of victim safety. There is no single person in the legal system whom advocates can approach to revamp the court's response to these cases. Each agency has to be brought into the process of change and each change in an individual agency has to be coordinated with the other agencies either affected by the change or necessary to make the change take place. (Pence, 1997, p. 36)

This statement above from one of Pence's unpublished writings on the Domestic Abuse Intervention Project (DAIP) explicates the 'complex system of agencies' (Pence, 1997, p. 92) that gets triggered by a victim of DASV seeking help, and the importance of how all these systems must be coordinated in tandem for change to occur. In her pioneering book (co-written with Micheal Paymar), *Education Groups for Men who Batter: The Duluth Model*, these words further illuminate this early systems change thinking on tackling domestic perpetration:

Organisers of DAIP found DAIP debated, cajoled, and negotiated with law enforcement agencies, the justice system, and human service providers to go beyond a superficial examination of the flaws in the system to committing to a comprehensive overhaul of the police, court, and human service systems' response to these cases. (Pence & Paymar, 1993, p. xiii)

In England and Wales, as a result of this systems approach and thinking, working with those who use violence and harmful behaviours through intervention programmes are now considered to be a vital component of the CCR to tackling DA (Price, 2016), and domestic violence perpetrator programmes (Phillips et al., 2013). Perhaps, threads from Pence's systems advocacy on multi-agency systems coordination in working with men who use harmful behaviours, can be found in the Multi-Agency Tasking And Coordination (MATAC), and Domestic Abuse Whole System Approach (DAWSA), which emphasises multi-agency partnerships, comprising criminal justice and community safety agencies coordinating and pooling resources to tackle the problem of serial perpetration of domestic abuse (Davies and Biddle, 2018).

Our Motivations as Editors

Our aim, through this book, is to demonstrate how system-oriented insights and ideas can be generated when we think in terms of 'systems'—whether in relation to theory, research, and practice. At the University of Suffolk, and since 2014, many of our domestic abuse evaluations have typically built on methodological pluralism principles as a core principle. These evaluations also involved many individuals and organisations with diverse views about 'what works, and for whom' (see Pawson & Tilley, 1997) around the thorny issues of domestic abuse, online harms, and childhood sexual abuse (CSA). As mentioned earlier, we had extensively applied Theory of Change/TOC (including running workshops with stakeholders) and used realist methods[11] (Contexts-Mechanisms-Organisations configurations) to evaluate interventions. And together with colleagues, applied an interdisciplinary ecological framework (inspired by Bronfenbrenner's socio-ecological theory), to assessing the Violence Against Women and Girls funding ecosystem (Adisa et al., 2020); and the structural violence experienced by victims-survivors with insecure immigration status (Adisa et al., 2021); and in online abuse and safeguarding in educational settings (Bond & Phippen, 2022; Phippen & Bond, 2020). Elsewhere, an ecological framework has also been applied to the government's Serious Violence Prevention strategy based on the WHO's public health approach, dubbed a 'whole-system multi-agency approach' (PHE, 2019). Essentially, in this ecological framework, interpersonal violence is viewed as the outcome of interaction among many factors at four distinct levels and systems—the individual, the relationship, and the community and the societal local systems, boundaries, systems within systems, actors, and stakeholders, respectively (WHO, 2018).

Through continuing questioning and reflection, we increasingly recognised the value (and limits) of conventional TOCs and how many of these evaluations are addressing symptoms rather than systemic root causes. The lack of attention given to the 'systemness' of change, systems

---

[11] Realist evaluation has been described as a 'distant cousin' to systems thinking (see Williams & Imam, 2007). The comprehensive edited volume by Williams and Imam was arguably the first attempt to bridge the gap between the field of systems thinking and evaluation.

leadership, or in understanding interconnected aspects of the wider systems-environment link, have inspired this book project, and indeed the individual authors who have contributed chapters.

This is not to say that the concept of systems thinking/approach does not have its own challenges, as we will discuss later in this introductory chapter, but by re-examining the pertinent systemic issues within DASV through this lens, our hope is that we might better be able to understand the elements that make systemic change challenging to achieve, how systems thinking might be used in a practical sense in this sphere, and for the first time, devoting an entire edited book collection to the purposeful use of critical systems thinking approaches to DASV. Additionally, we recognise that the language of systems dynamics (in relation to capturing changes over time, and across space) is also useful in thinking about long-term systems change, and we are limited by our retrospective case study approach.

At the beginning of the book project, we (as editors) were intentionally minimalist in the guidance and literature on systems provided to our brave co-authors (a mix of academics, policy professionals, and practitioners), in order to capture the breadth and depth of understandings and experiences. We are indeed most grateful to our authors, all of whom gracefully rose to the challenge. Most of the authors are not systems thinkers in the traditional sense and so this book provided an opportunity to mull over this concept of systems thinking into accessible forms that are applicable to the DASV setting. Over several months, we as editors undertook many one-to-one discussions with some of the authors to clarify the system concepts and to function as a sounding board for the application of systems approaches and concepts. This concept-building 'convening' helped to further imbibe a collaborative spirit in the process of sense-making (both in acting as editors and co-authors). In a sense, we created a system within a system, and used open and positive discussion feedback loops to refine these ideas. In each chapter, the authors signify their engagement with systems approaches in interesting and varied ways, paving way, we hope, for an interesting and enhanced reading.

In fact, one of the strengths of systems as a heuristic device is that it allows people to iteratively develop their emerging ideas and interpretations further into refined documents, and final papers. More importantly, it was our intention throughout this book, to foster dialogue, collaboration, and a pragmatic spirit among diverse authors in developing (and applying) the ideas in this book—to bring different voices to speak to the foundation building work of systems thinking and approaches in DASV sphere, which could be potentially applied to research, evaluation, policy, and practice. To have imposed theoretical and philosophical ideas on the authors right from the beginning would have been at odds with this principle.

One of the interesting and unique aspects of this book has been that all the case studies are retrospective illustrations of applied systems approaches, to potentially identify new lines of thinking as well as research, policy, and practice directions.

Our Approach to Editing and Curating the Diverse Chapters

One of the strengths of this collection is that our contributing authors come from different disciplines and/or use different methods and contexts (e.g. sociology, criminology, forensic psychology, education, safeguarding practice, policy)—and as Editors, we have extensive expertise in systems-oriented evaluations and violence and abuse. It should be noted that most of our authors came into this ambitious book project without explicitly applying systems approaches or even ever heard of critical systems thinking as a concept. We are grateful for their collaboration and openness to embark on this journey with us, as editors of the ultimate publication. In support of this endeavour, we also acted as co-authors in a few of the chapters (Adisa, in Chapters 3, and 5; Bond in Chapter 8). The common language of critical systems thinking has been used to signify and enhance the purposeful approach of engaging readers from different backgrounds to better identify the threads and ideas that are contained in this book.

For the reader, we hope that by the end of this book, that the value and promise of systems thinking and systems change in optimising efforts to tackle DASV[12] has provided ample 'food for thought' to take forward some of these ideas in your own research, developing and applying new theories, and for practice. We very much see this book as a starting point in activating conversations about systems thinking in loosening problem spaces (to use Davies' apt term) of domestic abuse and sexual violence.

Organisation of Chapters in the Book

This book contains insights based on our examination and applications of systems approach, and in Chapter 2, Richard Baldwin draws on his research findings to advocate for a re-energised multi-agency working approach through centring system-oriented meanings of community coordinated response for local systems change. The chapter introduces the concept of 'boundary spanners' to depict actors who help victims-survivors navigate the system.

In Chapter 3, Adisa is joined by Joana Ferreira, Margaret Hill, and Lisa Pack who explore the potential of a systems thinking approach in signifying and enhancing community-based systems change. The chapter also uses a well-known ecological framework to surface multi-level system blockages encountered (namely funding continuity issues and a bureaucratic tender process) that hinders systems change efforts.

Chapter 4 sees Carolyn Leader explore a socio-technical systems approach to researching technologically facilitated intimate abuse. Her chapter provides a convincing justification for a system thinking approach to ground further research within the field of technology-mediated intimate partner abuse.

The next chapter by Meena Kumari (with Adisa) fuses a notion of hope (*hopes for change*) with systems leadership to explore hopeful possibilities for systems change through sustained allyship, and meaningful systems visibility of Black, Brown, and other racially minoritised communities.

---

[12] We use the phrase 'DASV sphere' severally as more inclusive and diverse terms. However, in two of the chapters, the use of term Violence Against Women Girls/Domestic Abuse Sexual Violence (VAWG/DASV) sphere is also used interchangeably due to how the case study intervention has been named in policy.

Katherine Allen, in Chapter 6, analyses and reflects on a small-scale study undertaken with nine Rape Crisis Centre (RCC) workers from two English centres. Her chapter reflects on the parallels between critical systems thinking frameworks and feminist epistemic techniques, exploring how critical systems heuristics could be utilised by RCC training developers in order to be more responsive to local needs and contexts.

In Chapter 7, Emily Setty looks at the systems of preventing and responding to abusive image sharing among young people. She provides a socio-cultural perspective to develop an argument for a holistic approach to addressing the socio-cultural contextual causes of abusive image sharing. Suggestions are made for an improved systems response.

In Chapter 8, Katie Tyrrell and Andy Phippen (with Bond) turn to higher educational settings to look at systemic responses to online abuse on campuses. Systems theory approaches are rarely applied in online safeguarding contexts, and this case study is offered to meet this gap. The chapter uses authentic student voice to depict what needs to change across Higher Education institutional responses to online sexual and domestic abuse, and how outcomes for victims can be improved when effective and supportive systems are in place.

Criminal justice responses present a significant opportunity for bringing about systems change for the system to work better for victims-survivors. But a re-orientating towards a systems focus and systems advocacy approach is needed, and in Chapter 9, Mark Manning positions the policing of domestic abuse as a 'wicked problem', and explores through policy shifts and a values lens, whether the system structure of criminal justice agencies like the police and its relationship with the English legal system are compatible with the systemic changes that are necessary for an effective and formal rights-based experience for victims of crime. The chapter also offers some implications for policy and practice.

In this first volume, it is impracticable to do justice to the extensive wealth and breadth of systems approaches. All of the case studies used in this text take place in a UK setting, but we hope, still offers room for interesting international comparisons in future work. In future volumes, there is scope to present a cross-country exploration of systems approaches studies on DASV on aspects that have been highlighted as important through conversations with Domestic Abuse sector leaders, allowing for more ground to be covered in this purposeful documentation of systems thinking possibilities, and of its usefulness in theory building and practice on systems change.

Finally, in this volume, we have not included a concluding section intentionally, as our hope is that this foundational volume inspires energising conversations, and systems thinking inquiries (and encounters) in the violence and abuse sphere. It is our greatest hope that every reader that encounters this edited book collection is as inspired as we are to think in systems, both in its interconnected, collective, and relational sense. As the wisdom from the African proverb at the beginning of this chapter suggests, it doesn't matter if one is the tree, the bird or the forest, the point that we make throughout this collection is that the issues of DASV are interconnected and interdependent, through a complex systems change lens. At the very least, the treatment, given to the systems approach in this text, is an additional methodological skill and toolkit available to whatever DASV problem spaces that we may all find ourselves in, because domestic abuse (and sexual violence) is universally everyone's business.

Appendix

See Table 1.

Table 1 Terms, definitions and approach to applying the suggested theory-based systems framework (Adisa et al., 2023)

Terms	What it means
System boundaries	Describing the system and its wider context for sense-making. 'What is in, and what is out?'
Power and resource flows	The individual and collective power of actors within the system, and how system resources are controlled
Systems levers	Conditions and capacities for change (for example, policies, practices, relational dynamics, mental models)
Systems leadership	Systems leadership—skills, capacities and values for leading systems change (individual, community, institutions)
Systematic theory of change/Systemic theory of change*	Here we are interested in the degrees of certainty and agreement among key actors and stakeholders on system level impacts which calls for a theory of change that is characterised by a systems approach (systemic theory of change). However, for this specific domestic abuse evaluation project and in adapting the framework to a practical (and complex) setting, a systematic theory of change was implemented in line with Stroh's (2015) success amplification and goal achievement theory to surface 'what success looks like'
System structure	Drawing on the iceberg metaphor: identifying one or all system elements or subsystems that are visible and not so visible. The system structure can influence system behaviour
Complexity	Identifying aspects that make aspects of the intervention unpredictable and uncertain
Blueprint for continuity and change	Systems change is distinguished from episodic systems change, and commitment and investment is made to sustain change efforts into the long term

References

Adisa, O., Allen, K., & Ferreira, J. (2021). *Anchor+ evaluation.* Centre for Abuse Research. University of Suffolk.

Adisa, O., Allen, K., Kumari, M., Weir, R., & Bond, E. (2020). *Mapping the VAWG funding ecosystem in England and Wales. Project report.* Centre for Abuse Research. SISER.

Adisa, O., Allen, K., Manning, M., Ferreira, J. & Horvath, M. (2023). *Drive systems change evaluation: Final report.* Institute for Social Justice and Crime, University of Suffolk

Phippen. A., & Bond, E. (2020). *Online harassment and hate crime in HEIs—Report from FOI.* University of Suffolk.

Bond, E., & Phippen, A. (2022). *Safeguarding adults online: Perspectives on rights to participation.* Policy Press.

Boyle, K. (2019). What's in a name? Theorising the inter-relationships of gender and violence. *Feminist Theory, 20*(1), 19–36.

Brennan, I., Myhill, A., Tagliaferri, G., & Tapley, J. (2021). Policing a new domestic abuse crime: Effects of force-wide training on arrests for coercive control. *Policing and Society, 31*(10), 1153–1167.

Bronfenbrenner, U. (1979). *The ecology of human development.* Harvard University Press.

Cabrera, D., & Cabrera, L. (2015). *Systems thinking made simple.*

Cabrera, D., & Cabrera, L. (2022). DSRP theory: A primer. *Systems, 10*(2), 26.

Caffrey, L. (2017). The importance of perceived organisational goals: A systems thinking approach to understanding child safeguarding in the context of domestic abuse. *Child Abuse Review., 26*(5), 339–350.

Carey, G., Malbon, E., Carey, N., Joyce, A., Crammond, B., & Carey, A. (2015). Systems science and systems thinking for public health: A systematic review of the field. *BMJ Open, 5*(12), e009002.

Castellani, B., & Hafferty, F. W. (2009). *Sociology and complexity science: A new field of inquiry.* Springer.

Churchman, C. W. (1970). Operations research as a profession. *Management science, 17*(2), B-37.

Domestic Abuse Intervention Programmes. (n.d.). *Latest projects.* https://www.theduluthmodel.org/what-is-the-duluth-model/latest-projects/

Davies, L. (2016). Wicked problems: How complexity science helps direct education responses to preventing violent extremism. *Journal of Strategic Security, 9*(4), 32–52.

Davies, P. A., & Biddle, P. (2018). Implementing a perpetrator-focused partnership approach to tackling domestic abuse: The opportunities and challenges of criminal justice localism. *Criminology & Criminal Justice, 18*(4), 468–487. https://doi.org/10.1177/1748895817734590

Defra. (2021). *Defra theory of change toolkit—SD1421.* Department of Environment, Food and Rural Affairs.

Flood, R. L., & Jackson, M. C. (1991). *Critical systems thinking.* Wiley.

Flood, R. L., & Romm, N. R. A. (1997). *Critical systems thinking: Current research and practice.* Springer.

Foster-Fishman, P. G., & Behrens, T. R. (2007). Systems change reborn: Rethinking our theories, methods, and efforts in human services reform and community-based change. *American Journal of Community Psychology, 39*(3), 191–196.

Foster-Fishman, P. G., Nowell, B., & Yang, H. (2007). Putting the system back into systems change: A framework for understanding and changing organizational and community systems. *American Journal of Community Psychology, 39*(3), 197–215. https://doi.org/10.1007/s10464-007-9109-0

Giddens, A. (1986). *The constitution of society: Outline of the theory of structuration* (Vol. 349). University of California Press.

Hester, M. (2011). The three planet model: Towards an understanding of contradictions in approaches to women and children's safety in contexts of domestic violence. *The British Journal of Social Work, 41*(5), 837–853.

Imam, I., LaGoy, A., & Williams, B. (2007). Introduction. In: Williams B., & Imam, I. (Eds.), *Systems concepts in evaluation: An expert anthology.* California Edge Press/American Evaluation Association.

Jackson, M. C. (2019). *Critical systems thinking and the management of complexity.* Wiley.

Kelly, L. (1987). The continuum of sexual violence. In *Women, violence and social control* (pp. 46–60). Springer.

Kelly, L. (1988). *Surviving sexual violence.* Polity Press.

Kelly, L. (2016). The conducive context of violence against women and girls. *Discover Society, 1.* https://discoversociety.org/2016/03/01/theorising-violence-against-women-and-girls/

Meadows, D. H. (2008). *Thinking in systems: A primer.* Chelsea Green Publishing.

Midgley, G. (2001). *Systemic intervention: Philosophy, methodology, and practice.* Springer Science & Business Media.

Munro, E. (2005). A systems approach to investigating child abuse deaths. *British Journal of Social Work, 35*(4), 531–546.

Newell, A., & Simon, H. A. (1972). *Human problem solving* (Vol. 104). Prentice-hall Englewood Cliffs, NJ.

Orr, J. M., Leider, J. P., & Gutilla, M. J. (2023). System approaches in governmental public health: Findings from an analysis of the literature. *Systems Research and Behavioral Science, 40*(1), 159–169.

Pawson, R., & Tilley, N. (1997). *Realist evaluation.* Sage.

Pence, E., & Paymar, M. (1993). *Education groups for men who batter: The Duluth model.* Springer Publishing Company.

Pence. (1997). *Safety for battered women in a textually mediated legal system* (Unpublished Doctoral dissertation). www.praxisinternational.org

Phillips, R., Kelly, L., & Westmarland, N. (2013). *Domestic violence perpetrator programmes: An historical overview.*

Public Health England. (2019). *A whole-system multi-agency approach to serious violence prevention. A resource for local system leaders in England.* HM Government.

Price, P. (2016). Working Trans-culturally with Domestically Violent Men. Moving in the Shadows: Violence in the Lives of Minority Women and Children, 245.

Rittel, H. W., & Webber, M. M. (1973). Dilemmas in a general theory of planning. *Policy Sciences, 4*(2), 155–169.

Safelives. (2018). *Domestic abuse matters: Police responders and champions training.*

Stanton, M., & Welsh, R. (2012). Systemic thinking in couple and family psychology research and practice. *Couple and Family Psychology: Research and Practice, 1*(1), 14.

Stroh, D. P. (2015). *Systems thinking for social change: A practical guide to solving complex problems, avoiding unintended consequences, and achieving lasting results.* Chelsea Green Publishing.

Ulrich, W. (1996). *A primer to critical systems heuristics for action researchers.* Centre for Systems Studies.

Ulrich, W. (2005). *A brief introduction to critical systems heuristics (CSH).* ECOSENSUS project site.

UN. (2017). *United nations system leadership framework.* CEB UN System Chief Executives Board for Coordination.

UN. (2018). *Inclusive systemic evaluation for gender equality, Environments and Marginalized voices (ISE4GEMs): A new approach for the SDG era.* https://www.unwomen.org/en/digital-library/publications/2018/9/ise4gems-a-new-approach-for-the-sdg-era#:~:text=Accordingly%2C%20the%20UN%20Women%20Independent,evaluation%20practice%20with%20intersectional%20analysis

Vickers, G. (1983). *Human systems are different.* Harper & Row.

World Health Organization. (2018). *Violence prevention alliance.* World Health Organization. https://www.who.int/groups/violence-prevention-alliance/approach

Wan, P. Y.-Z. (2013). *Reframing the social: Emergentist systemism and social theory.* Ashgate Publishing, Ltd.

Williams, B., & Imam, I. (2007). *Systems concepts in evaluation: An expert anthology.* EdgePress of Inverness.

Multi-Agency and Community-Based Systems Responses and Applications

A Systems Approach Analysis of a Multi-Agency Response to Domestic Abuse

Richard Baldwin

Introduction

'We are all boundary spanners now'—Paul Williams 2013. Partnerships and networks have recently been important in the face of public sector cuts and state fragmentation, but they are also particularly significant in shaping public sector responses to 'wicked issues' such as domestic abuse. Head and Alford (2015, p. 712) define a 'wicked issue' as '…. complex, unpredictable, open ended, or intractable'. Such societal problems are too complex to be addressed by one single organisation and require a collaborative, societal response which doesn't start and finish with the

R. Baldwin (✉)
Colchester, Essex, UK
e-mail: rb.systemchange@gmail.com

© The Author(s), under exclusive license to Springer Nature
Switzerland AG 2024
O. Adisa and E. Bond (eds.), *Tackling Domestic Abuse and Sexual Violence*, Palgrave
Studies in Victims and Victimology, https://doi.org/10.1007/978-3-031-58600-2_2

criminal justice system or victim[1] advocacy but is genuinely joined up with everyone playing their part.

A shift in response requires systems change PG Foster-Fishman et al. (2007) describes this as '....an intentional process designed to alter the status quo by shifting and realigning the form and function of a targeted system'. This goes far beyond the assumption that organisations should simply work more closely together.

However, there are considerable barriers to system change which include limited capacity and resources, organisational cultures and jurisdictions, competition, trust, communication along with misaligned objectives. Such substantial challenges can often lead to duplication, inefficiencies, and gaps in service provision, leaving victims of domestic abuse baffled at a time when they require safety, clarity and a system response paced to match their individual journey.

This chapter seeks to explore the complexities of multi-agency working and system change in tackling domestic abuse. Firstly, looking at previous research and unpicking the evolution of the response to domestic abuse from partnership working, collaboration and system coordination, reinforcing the need for advocacy in the form of a 'boundary spanner' to help navigate the system as well as the advantages of a community response. The chapter then looks at a case study of the arrangements in a two-tier county in England, which includes insights from commissioners and practitioners on how the current system is or in some cases isn't working. The chapter is limited to system support for victims and leaves the debates around perpetrator support for another day.

To provide a framework for the chapter several papers have been studied as part of a wider literature review to aid the analysis of a multi-agency response to domestic abuse as well as the complexities and the difficulties that exist in system change. Literature reviewed frames domestic abuse as a wicked issue and considers the origins of domestic abuse support, the move away from feminist advocacy towards

---

[1] At times I use gendered language in recognition of the gendered bias of domestic abuse, but I recognise that men are also subject to abuse with the impacts equally devastating. In addition, I use the term victim, survivor, and client interchangeably depending on the language used by those I have interviewed and depending upon the circumstances being described.

a more formal, criminal justice stance and the consequences of this for victim support. Unpicking the intricacies of multi-agency working, and the tensions and contradictions which exist between organisations is explored, along with how the evolution of system thinking and as such support helps victims.

Multi-Agency Response and System Change

According to Sullivan and Skelcher (2002, p. 1), a multi-organisational partnership is—'a formal expression of shared commitment to act in the common interest. Partnership is about sharing responsibility and overcoming the inflexibility created by organisational, sectoral, and geographical boundaries'.

There are of course power dynamics at play too especially when it comes to the allocation of resources. Concerns around unequal power dynamics in partnership arrangements to bid for funding were highlighted in research undertaken by the University of Suffolk in 2020 to map VAWG funding with one survey participant stating that '...*partnerships can enable organisations to bring their own specialist activity to benefit a wider client group, but it sometimes feels as though larger organisations are using smaller charities like ours to add value to their bid, without really sharing the funding benefits, so that we end [up] subsidising the bid*'. Adisa et al. (2020, p. 42), S. Javdani and N. E. Allen (2011) also establish that shared power in decision-making is empowering for both individuals and organisations.

However, is this need for collaboration in responding to wicked issues such as domestic abuse a wicked issue in itself? Adrian Webb (1991, p. 229) recognises the need for systematic and well-ordered responses but argues that ... 'the reality is all too often a jumble of services fractionalised by professional, cultural and organisational boundaries and tiers of governance'.

Williams (2013) acknowledges that the requirement for people and organisations to work across both specialist areas along with organisational and even sectoral boundaries has become an established feature of UK public policy. Van Meerkeek and Ebenbos (2019) go further describing the changing nature of public management and governance in response to the challenges of modern societies, noting a 'torrent' of complex and cross-boundary wicked issues.

Harwin et al. (1999, p. 292) '…. consider the complexities that the woman faces when she tries to get help. It may be crucial to her success in escaping violence (or even surviving it) that the local housing department, police, health services, and other agencies from whom she seeks support, work together effectively'.

Before looking in more detail at the benefits and challenges of a multi-agency response, considering where the governance of domestic abuse sits provides some useful insights into why and how the current arrangements have been formed and helps explain some of the unintended consequences and tensions that may have occurred as a result. Davies (2018) takes us back to the introduction of local Crime and Disorder Reduction Partnerships in the late 1990s which placed domestic abuse firmly in the criminal justice space. Law enforcement and justice play an essential part in any criminal act, but Harvie and Manzi (2011, p. 91) discuss three dominant discourses: criminal justice, managerialism, and equalities. They propose that by framing domestic abuse as a criminal justice issue, a culture of performance management and a redefinition of equality from domestic abuse being a gendered issue to equality of opportunity to support have taken the issue away from the core issue of male power and control, changing the 'ideological direction from feminism towards legalism and bureaucratic processes'. Hughes et al. (2001) argue that the 'messy' needs of survivors can often be ignored in favour of measurable indicators. The introduction of Victim Support in 2004, as a blanket, universal service for any victim of crime placed specialist domestic abuse support on the fringes of government support, having to compete against all other crime and disorder issues.

Vinton and Wilke (2014 p. 716) ask if 'collaborations are enough'? arguing that victims need 'protection as well as necessary resources such as housing, food, clothing, legal assistance, advocacy, legal representation, mental health services, educational services, job training, health care and children's services'. Unlike some instances of collaboration, exercised in response to domestic abuse, it does not exist in a vacuum, it happens in a dynamic environment which can often have limitations.

The Coordinated Community Response

The national charity Standing Together in their publication 'In Search of Excellence' (2020, p. 6) describes a coordinated community response as '…. shifting responsibility for safety away from individual survivors to the community and services existing to support them'.

Cleaver et al. (2019, p. 152) highlight several cases where approaches that adopt an '…advocacy rather than criminal justice framework may be more effective in encouraging victims to report abuse, thereby potentially enabling earlier interventions'. Research has indicated that women experiencing abuse more often reach out to friends, family members, neighbours, and colleagues rather than professionals (Ansara & Hindin, 2011; Parker & Lee, 2002). These 'Informal supporters' often know these abusive situations best and although informal support is no replacement for specialist support it can be an essential route into professional help. Encouraging communities to demonstrate unity with those suffering domestic abuse has the potential to bring hidden issues to light, helping to frame this wicked issue as a societal, community problem rather than a criminal justice one. Gregory and Williamson (2021, p. 1) and Kulkarni et al. (2012, p. 97) argue that service delivery based around 'active listening, a supportive presence and empowerment' are at times undervalued within the wider response.

The Importance of Boundary Spanners

With a multitude of organisations all trying to do their best to support victims of domestic abuse, there may be overlap, fragmentation, duplication and inefficiency. The need for someone skilled in working through partnerships and networks is best described within the concept of 'boundary spanners'. Whether that be in a dedicated role or embedded within elements of an existing position, the potential contribution of skilled 'boundary spanners' is immense. Boundary spanners need to have the strategic and operational knowledge of the project and are the glue which holds things together, as a coordinator, facilitator, negotiator, problem solver and analyst.

Van Meerkeek and Edenbos (2019, p. 646) usefully describe a '...scaffolding of a myriad number of boundaries, including organisational, professional, social, cultural and psychological...they interweave together to form complex policy spaces'. They go on to propose that boundary spanning has become a core activity of modern public management.

Often all eyes will turn to the boundary spanner as a lynch pin where there is work to do or an issue to iron out. The system response to wicked issues has someone to unpick its complexities in the form of a boundary spanner. But how do victims of domestic abuse unpick that complex response? Everyone is trying to help, all with a part to play, but arguably the victim may often themselves have to take on that boundary-spanning role to ensure that they receive the right support. At point of crisis, this can be a step too far for people, resulting in withdrawing from support all together. In a worst-case scenario for a domestic abuse victim this may mean returning to the perpetrator, significantly heightening risk. If we add in additional challenges around mental health, substance dependency, financial hardship and parenting, the landscape becomes even harder to navigate. The more challenges, the greater number of agencies supporting the individual.

Local Systems Perspective

Views on the current system response to domestic abuse were sought from key strategic and operational stakeholders working in the field of domestic abuse in a two-tier local authority county, providing first-hand examples of how multi-agency arrangements work locally as well as insights into the contradictions, challenges faced, and improvements required. The list of interviewees can be found in the Reference section of this chapter.

Five main themes have been identified in their responses; specialist advocacy versus statutory services; barriers to support; governance; boundary spanners; and a move to a coordinated community response.

Specialist Advocacy Versus Statutory Responsibilities

It can be a knife edge of safeguarding and victim led practice. (I5)

At time of crisis, survivors of domestic abuse may need support from a wide range of agencies both statutory and voluntary. Front-line specialist support workers talked about the need to build a relationship with the client, describing it as a foundation for all future work, getting to know the level of risk posed by the offender, as well as 'understanding what the individual requires from the support on offer' (I8). It is also important here to set 'clear professional boundaries and clear expectations on what the client can expect from the service' (I9). There is a recognition from support services that timing is everything, one specialist support service describing it as the client needing to be 'ready, willing, and able' to accept the support being offered and for some the timing may not be right, but the importance here was that they knew the door is always open for them to return (I10).

There is inevitably a spectrum of complexity with some clients having substantial mental health and substance dependency needs, further adding to the number of support organisations involved in that individual's journey or recovery plan. With so many people required to build the puzzle of support, some front-line workers talked about a period of 'temporary disempowerment' (I8), whereby in some cases it was required for the support worker to take responsibility and decision-making away from the client to help them make sense of the plethora of appointments and people involved in supporting them. Although the term 'temporary disempowerment' is used, on reflection I would argue that this is more a case of the support worker taking on a boundary spanner role, akin to a ringmaster at the circus.

When asked the question of how interviewees' organisations work in a person-centred way it became clear that not all agencies can be led by the victim. The police, as an example, have the primary responsibility to investigate crime, and in some instances the risk to the victim may be so great that they will have an obligation to take positive action against a perpetrator, maybe against the wishes of the victim. This has ramifications where, for example, the perpetrator is also the main carer for the victim, whereby a care package must be hurriedly arranged, again often against the direct wishes of the victim (I4). Similarly, children's social care has a statutory responsibility to protect children, if they consider the risk to a child to be so great if that abusive relationship continues then they may have no alternative than to take a child into temporary care, almost certainly against the wishes of the victim. One safeguarding professional said that people absolutely have the right to choose what decisions they make '…but if a child's welfare is at risk, then those decisions may need to be temporarily taken out of their hands' (I5). However, no victim can make a rational decision to leave an abusive relationship if they feel their lives are at risk and fear a lack of protection if they make the decision to leave or to prosecute (I3).

This helps to highlight that those different agencies have different responsibilities and jurisdictions in each given circumstance, which in some instances cannot be victim led. This dichotomy was appreciated and understood by all those I interviewed.

Barriers to Accessing Support

Adding complexity and further fragmentation. (I2)

Much discussion has been had both nationally and locally about the need for, what is described as, 'by and for services' as a way to ensuring that services meet the needs of victims, especially those with protected characteristics (Home Office VAWG Strategy, 2021). As an example, someone from the LGBTQ+ community is far more likely to understand the needs of a LGBTQ+ victim, whether that be the barriers they face in seeking support or the support they may need itself. This is true of male victims, disabled victims, or victims from racialised communities. There was general recognition from those interviewed that this was an important feature of support, somewhat missing in the county and more needed to be done to understand the barriers to accessing support and make collective efforts to remove those barriers. The difficulty then highlighted was 'what do you do in a rural county, which isn't particularly diverse?' (I2). It would almost be impossible to establish support services in that way due to the small numbers of victims with those protected characteristics, highlighting the need for culturally responsive provision to be embedded within mainstream services.

It was universally agreed that no-one should be denied support but embedding specialist caseworkers within services seemed the most agreeable solution in the absence of a 'by and for' service model in every area which was felt unrealistic. One area of concern which was highlighted amongst practitioners at interview was the lack of support for victims with No Recourse to Public Funds (NRPFs) (I1, I7). Another area of concern expressed by all those interviewed was the lack of support for people with complex mental health needs. 'We shouldn't be surprised that victims who have been subject to such trauma, some for many many years should need support with their mental health' (I6). Yet, it may take months for any type of trauma therapy to be forthcoming. Additionally, it was felt that mental health services at a strategic level had so far not been involved in the multi-agency response to domestic abuse with the lack of resources and underfunding identified as the major reason (I1, I2, I3, I6).

Strategic Governance

A necessary evil. (I6)

Those interviewed talked about governance as 'inevitably losing sight of individuals' (I8) and whilst it was felt that the 'system strategically works well in many ways.... there is a disconnect between strategic plans and what happens operationally' (I9). This was evident, as interviewees working at a commissioning level had a greater understanding of the strategy and governance arrangements in place, whereas at an operational level there was less knowledge or even interest in governance as the focus of discussion was naturally more about working with the victims or survivors. It was felt that opportunities to come together as a system responding to domestic abuse were hugely beneficial, but more could be done to use victim voice at all levels, as well as using the testimony of victims' journeys through the system to shape future service provision.

The need for strong political leadership was one which often came up amongst those working in a political environment. It was felt that although on the whole services worked well together with agreed pathways, having three separate organisations (IDVA, Outreach and Victim Care) commissioned based on victim risk was far from ideal with a solution offered by some supporting victims to 'put all the money in one pot and commission according to what's required' (I9). There was recognition that progress had been made in aligning commissioning between local councils and the Police and Crime Commissioner (I1, I2) but concerns remained amongst specialist support services that competitive commissioning inevitably resulted in organisations being less likely to collaborate and share best practice in order to protect their organisations (I9). Some interviewees noted the previous ambition to create a 'coordination centre' for domestic abuse services which would provide one route into support as well as a shared case management system, which was felt would be beneficial (I2, I3, I7). There was significant divergence of views between the benefits of a universal, countywide service such as the Outreach Service, where everyone could signpost to one place for support against those services based in localities. Arguably by services being based in specific localities, they are more linked into the support structure required for victims, such as housing officers, schools, family support practitioners, for example, and thus more equipped to meet the direct needs of individuals. All those interviewed cited 'relationships' as the single most important feature of multi-agency working, with collaborative work more likely to take place where people knew one another and had worked with each other for many years.

Boundary Spanners

Communication key to successful partnerships, relationships and support. (I10)

I was interested to understand whether specialist supports services, in their role as victim advocates saw themselves as boundary spanners at an operational level and although many were unfamiliar with the academic term, recognised that they played that role on the victims' behalf, coordinating various services to ensure that the victims individual needs are met. There was, however, some concern expressed about having to 'handover' victims to other services when risk was reduced, for example (I8, I9, I10). We have previously established that building a relationship with the victim is key and as such having to signpost on to another service added to the system being disjointed but also gave the opportunity for victims to opt out of support and in extreme cases return to an abusive relationship. Placing the added pressure on victims to tell their story and explain their needs to yet another professional and to once again build a relationship adds to the need for one advocate supporting the victim throughout their entire journey, being led by them and ultimately resulting in better person-centred outcomes (I8, I9, I10). When we consider partnership data from safe accommodation providers; housing, health, finance and legal are the top four areas where people require additional support, this further helps to demonstrate the complexity if you imagine victims having to work with practitioners in all those areas, simultaneously while recovering from significant recent trauma.

The role of a boundary spanner in helping to coordinate the multi-agency response at a strategic level was also seen as important across all the interviews undertaken. There was, however, some concern that if one organisation pays for and hosts that boundary-spanning officer, other organisations can then remove themselves from their responsibility to input either assuming that issues are 'covered' by the hosting organisation or even more concerning not fully taking part as the hosting organisation may be seen as taking the advantage politically (I1). The obvious solution here is to have a boundary spanner role which is paid for by an equal contribution from each partner organisation and where there is genuine buy-in at a political and senior officer level for all organisations to equally contribute.

The importance of skills in identifying and recruiting to a boundary spanner role at both an operational and strategic level cannot be under-estimated. Getting the right person who can work across organisational boundaries, culture and politics, remaining independent, yet at the same time calling partner organisations to account is paramount (I1, I6, I7).

When we consider the recommendations from Domestic Homicide Reviews, of the local cases a need for strong governance, training and communication have previously been highlighted along with engage-ment with multi-agency meetings such as the Multi-Agency Risk Assess-ment Conferences (MARAC). However, none of the cases I have reviewed reflected in depth on the complexity of a multi-agency response to domestic abuse or the barriers to working in a person-centred way instead focusing on recommendations for individual organisations or public awareness raising. There was mention of communication between agencies but nothing which showed the conflicts encountered in supporting victims, which I found surprising given what has been established through both the literature review and interviews. Equally interesting was the lack of focus on perpetrators, with a preferred focus on how the system could have reduced the risk to the victim.

Overwhelmingly all those interviewed identified communication as key to successful relationships, whether that be in direct support of the victim or between the various organisations.

Community Response

Harness the support of friends, family members and work colleagues. (I10)

Whilst the focus of interviews was on the specialist and statutory support available to victims of domestic abuse many people noted the important role friends and family members play in the initial disclosure and encouraging people to seek specialist support. Many will be aware of abusive behaviours and may have the opportunity to speak candidly with loved ones about their concerns, and whilst those interviewed recognised the precarious position this may put a friend or family member in, with some guidance it could mean that victims seek to safely leave an abusive relationship earlier. It was recognised that in an effort to make domestic abuse everyone's business, there was a need for more awareness raising and recognition across society as a whole on what the 'right response' to a disclosure or encouraging a disclosure may look and sound like.

A response rooted in community efficacy feels like it is gathering pace. Based on my research and findings I would propose that placing domestic abuse in a criminal justice setting can lose the person-centred approach due to its governance, politics and over management but this could be counteracted in the future by placing domestic abuse as a societal issue within our communities and one which can only be resolved with the help of friends, family, work colleagues and the wider community.

Conclusion

The complexities of domestic abuse require not only partners to work closely together and collaborate in their response but in many instances require system change.

Tensions inevitably exist between organisations supporting victims and the fact that where statutory safeguarding obligations exist it may not always be possible to be led by the needs and wishes of the victim. The need for a boundary spanner role both strategically and operationally has been highlighted and although support services did not describe themselves as such, the lack of an advocate leaves victims having to take on this role themselves, which is often overwhelming at a time when they just want the abuse to stop and to be safe. This support for the victim must be time limited with the ultimate aim being to empower victims to make their own decisions and choices.

We know that organisational jurisdictions can create fragmentation and barriers to person-centred responses but building relationships between organisations was mentioned as essential but the way in which services are commissioned and funded was cited as creating a competitive environment amongst support services resulting in less willingness to work in partnership and create those relationships.

A coordinated community response offers the best opportunity for future multi-agency working in supporting victims. Listening, believing, validating, and giving people time, time to build a supportive relationship, time to just be safe and time to reflect and rebuild are vital ingredients for catalysing a coordinated systemic response to domestic abuse.

References

Interviewee List

Interviews have been undertaken with people in the following organisations:

(I1) Public Health—commission safe accommodation and a domestic abuse outreach service. They also provide system wide strategic coordination.

(I2) Office of the Police and Crime Commissioner (OPCC)—The Office of the Police and Crime Commissioner (OPCC) has the responsibility for specialist support for victims of crime and as such commissions the countywide Independent Domestic Violence Advisor (IDVA) service for high-risk domestic abuse victims as well as Victim Care (VC) available for any victim of crime. The OPCC also provides strategic direction on policy for the constabulary.

(I3) Police—Responsibility for emergency response and investigating domestic abuse associated crimes but have a highly trained, dedicated team to support victims. They are also an active member of the Multi Agency Safeguarding Hub (MASH) as well as leading the Multi Agency Risk Assessment Conference (MARAC) process.

(I4) Safeguarding—Statutory responsibilities to safeguard adults.

(I5) Safeguarding—Statutory responsibilities to safeguard children.

(I6) Integrated Care System—The ICS work closely with GPs and Hospitals with the Safeguarding Lead advising on any safeguarding concerns people may have.

(I7) Housing Officers Group—Representatives from Housing Options Teams across come together to consider and resolve countywide reciprocal housing arrangements.

(I8) Outreach Support—The Domestic Abuse Outreach Service provides support to victims of domestic abuse and their children by assessing risk, drawing up safety plans and providing advocacy. Support is provided by a specialist trained team of outreach workers.

(I9) Specialist Support Services—Providing a range of services for victims of domestic abuse.

(I10) Specialist Support Services—Providing a range of services for victims of domestic abuse.

* * *

Adisa, O., et al. (2020). *Mapping VAWG funding ecosystem* (pp. 41–45). University of Suffolk.

Ansara, D. L., & Hindin, M. J. (2011). Psychosocial consequences of intimate partner violence for women and men in Canada. *Journal of Interpersonal Violence, 26*(8).

Cleaver, K., Maras, P., Oram, C., & McCallum, K. (2019). A review of UK based multi-agency approaches to early intervention in domestic abuse: Lessons to be learnt from existing evaluation studies. *Aggressive and Violent Behaviour, 46*, 140–155. Elsevier Ltd.

Davies, P. (2018). Tackling domestic abuse locally: Paradigms, ideologies and the political tensions of multi-agency working. *Journal of Gender-Based Violence, 2*(3), 429–446.

Foster-Fishman, P. G., Nowell, B., & Yang, H. (2007). *Putting the system back into systems change: A framework for understanding and changing organizational and community systems.* Springer Publishing

Gregory, A., & Williamson, E. (2021). 'I think it just made everything very much more intense': A qualitative secondary analysis exploring the role of friends and family providing support to survivors of domestic abuse during the COVID-19 Pandemic. *Journal of Family Violence.* Springer

Harvie, P., & Manzi, T. (2011), Interpreting multi-agency partnerships: Ideology, discourse and domestic violence. *Social and Legal Studies, 20*(1), 79–95. Sage Publishing.

Harwin, N., et al. (1999). *The multi-agency approach to domestic violence: New opportunities, old challenges.* Whiting and Birch.

Head, B. W., & Alford, J. (2015). Wicked problems: Implications for public policy and management. *Administration and Society, 47*, 711–739. Sage Publishing.

Home Office. (2021). *VAWG strategy*. Tackling violence against women and girls strategy—GOV.UK. www.gov.uk. Accessed 1 August 2021.

Hughes, H., Graham-Bermann, S., & Gruber, G. (2001). Resilience in children exposed to domestic. *The future of research, intervention and social policy, American psychological society* (pp. 67–90). Washington, DC.

Javdani, S., & Allen, N. E. (2011). *Councils as empowering contexts: Mobilizing the front line to foster systems change in the response to intimate partner violence.* Springer Publishing.

Kulkarni, S. J., Bell, H., & Rhodes, D. M. (2012), Back to basics: Essential qualities of services for survivors of intimate partner violence. *Violence Against Women, 18*(1), 85–101. Sage Publishing.

Parker, G., & Lee, C. (2002). Violence and abuse: An assessment of mid-aged Australian women's experiences. *Australian Psychologist, 37*(2), 142–148.

Sullivan, H. & Skelcher C. (2002). *Working across boundaries: Collaboration in Public Services.* Macmillan Education.

Standing Together. (2020). *In search of excellence.*

Van Meerkeek and Edenbos (2019). The life and times of a boundary spanner. *Journal of Public Administration Research and Theory, 29*(4), 646–648. Edward Elgar Publishing.

Vinton, L., & Wilke, D. (2014). Are collaborations enough? Professionals' knowledge of victim services. *Violence against Women, 20*(6), 716–729.

Webb, A. (1991). Coordination: A problem in public sector management. *Policy and Politics, 19*(4), 229–241.

Williams, P. (2013). We are all boundary spanners now. *International Journal of Public Sector Management, 26*(1), 17–32. Emerald Group Publishing Ltd.

Promoting Better Outcomes for Migrant Victim-Survivors Through Community-Based Systems Interactions and Levers of Change

Olumide Adisa, Joana Ferreira, Margaret Hill, and Lisa Pack

Introduction

The life of a victim-survivor with insecure migrant status in England and Wales is challenging. As the story of Julia shows:

O. Adisa (✉)
University of Suffolk, Ipswich, UK
e-mail: o.adisa@uos.ac.uk

J. Ferreira
University of Bath, Bath, UK
e-mail: jmgf21@bath.ac.uk

M. Hill · L. Pack
Leeway Domestic Violence and Abuse Services, Norwich, UK
e-mail: m.hill@leewaynwa.org.uk

L. Pack
e-mail: l.pack@leewaynwa.org.uk

© The Author(s), under exclusive license to Springer Nature   **49**
Switzerland AG 2024
O. Adisa and E. Bond (eds.), *Tackling Domestic Abuse and Sexual Violence*, Palgrave
Studies in Victims and Victimology, https://doi.org/10.1007/978-3-031-58600-2_3

Julia[1] has lived in [a county][2] for the last 4 years, moving here from Lithuania with her husband and her two children. Life had become difficult in Lithuania for the couple, and they moved to the UK for a new start, a fresh start. And it was a fresh start for a short time but then abuse that Julia's husband had promised her would stop when they moved started again here in the UK. Julia's husband was physically, emotionally, and financially controlling and abusive towards her. After 4 years Julia decided that she would ask for help, and she went to her local housing options team to ask for that help. She brought with her two children and a small bag of belongings she had packed. The abuse Julia and her children were experiencing had escalated to a point that Julia feared for her life and her children's life. The Housing Options team rang an out of county refuge for Julia—Julia was told that as she would not qualify for housing benefit so she would not be able to access an emergency bed in a refuge. *She was told she had 'NRPF' and that there was no support available for her.*

Broader immigration legislation, such as the No Recourse to Public Funds (NRPF) clause, adds further layers of disadvantage. This stipulation is defined under Section 115 of the Immigration and Asylum Act 1999 and was part of 'an array of measurements intended to close immigration routes into the UK' (Anitha, 2010, p. 463). Discriminatory and hostile policies create further barriers to migrants' access to support, safety, and justice. In the UK, such barriers have been made more visible by recent manifestations of the historical and systemic 'overlooking' of victimised migrants.

Another key example is the new Domestic Abuse Act 2022. This long-awaited legislation, which promised to set in stone systems of support and protection for victims of domestic abuse, was heavily criticised by third sector VAWG (Violence Against Women and Girls) organisations for its failure to make provisions to tackle the multiple forms of disadvantage and oppression migrant victims experience. The Act overlooks provisions in the Istanbul Convention which are designed to safeguard

[1] Real name and country of origin have been changed.
[2] For practical reasons, we have anonymised the names of the counties and instead in this paper, refer to the locations as 'a/the county' or 'the counties'.

the rights of migrant victim-survivors and leaves migrant women without assured access to support and safety.

Previous research has consistently demonstrated that migrant women are exposed to several specific stressors that shape their responses to and attitudes towards domestic abuse, while creating intersecting and intricate barriers to their pursuit of safety (Erez et al., 2009; Orloff & Garcia, 2013). For instance, unfamiliarity with available systems and legal rights within the host country can exacerbate women's vulnerability to controlling and abusive behaviour. The impact of victims' immigration and/ or residency status is equally crucial. Those with irregular or unstable immigration status are recognisably vulnerable to added forms of abuse and control (DAC, 2021; Erez et al., 2009), such as the threat of deportation—recently named as 'immigration abuse' (DAC, 2021). Even for those with regularised status, vulnerability persists if such status is dependent on the abusive partner (Erez et al., 2009; Raj & Silverman, 2002; Salcido & Adelman, 2004), and they are left choosing between abuse and the possibility of expulsion from the country.

The Domestic Abuse Commissioner (DAC)'s report *Safety before Status* found that migrant victim-survivors in England and Wales are often unable to (or refused) access to support (e.g. refuge accommodation) even when eligible, due to services wrongly assuming they were unable to do so due to their immigration status (DAC, 2021).

These migrant-specific stressors are situated within existing sources of oppression and disadvantage, such as the precarious VAWG funding landscape which increasingly limits organisations' ability to provide support services to marginalised populations (Adisa et al., 2020), as well as the patriarchal social context in which violence against women is perpetuated.

The DAC report further highlighted the various needs of domestic abuse victim-survivors, including 'immediate safety, basic physical needs, emotional support and navigating the legal processes relevant to their circumstances' (DAC, 2022a, p. 6). Importantly, this research found that victim-survivors faced several barriers in their attempts to access necessary support, with 'fewer than half of victims and survivors [...] able to access the community-based support that they wanted, and only 35% said accessing help was easy or straightforward' (DAC, 2022b, p. 2).

Community-based systems of support remain a vital pathway to safety. The story of Julia and others like hers, inspired the coordinated community efforts that culminated in an intervention specifically designed to support migrant victims-survivors in the two counties in England. This paper discusses the community-based system interactions and levers that led to the development and funding of the intervention.

Our Approach

Our case study is framed as a systemic intervention[3] and our choice for selecting this study to explore systems concepts and ideas retrospectively. It also describes the theoretical frameworks which have been adopted in this chapter, and which we have applied in two ways: (1) in depicting an interconnected system of support for migrant victims-survivors; (2) to uncover the community-based system dynamics which shaped the development, implementation, and evaluation of the case study.

We had all been involved in the three-year evaluation[4] and have undertaken other similar research projects seperately on the topic of migrant victims and survivors (see Adisa, 2019; DAC, 2021; Ferreira, 2021).

We purport that a retrospective exploration of the potential of systems thinking in community-based system change makes it an interesting case study to revisit. In this chapter, (the case study as a systemic intervention, affords a snapshot view of the perspectives which are typically marginalised; from top-down policy making via the 'hostile environment', down to the decisions of bureaucrats working in the statutory sector.

Systemic intervention is a methodologically pragmatic and pluralist approach which enables stakeholders, including researchers and independent evaluators, to critically interrogate the assumptions and value

---

[3] A systemic intervention can be defined as interventions that transcend a component-by-component approach due to the interconnectedness of phenomenon, which can be experienced globally and locally (Midgley, 2001). So-called wicked problems (as per Rittel & Webber, 1973), like domestic abuse, are more amenable to interventions that are systemic.

[4] The full independent evaluation team included Dr Katherine Allen, and she provided useful comments on an earlier draft of this chapter.

judgements that underlie different perspectives on a situation, with the aim of engendering change (Midgley, 2001).

Our aim is not to repeat the findings of the evaluation here in relation to intended programme outcomes and impacts of the intervention. Here in this chapter, we revisit our evidence base gathered through the evaluation and draw on our reflections to uncover the system interactions, levers of change, and actors within it. To support our recollections, we use the evidence base on the evaluation (as well as interviews with 31 professionals[5]) across the system.

Critical Systems Thinking Concepts Adopted

To describe the contextual and systemic issues relating to systems of support for migrant victims-survivors, we apply Bronfenbrenner's (1979) model of ecology. Bronfenbrenner (1979) proposed a novel model of human development focusing on the development of the person, their environment, and the interaction between the two. The ecological model seeks to move beyond simplistic models, understanding the 'ecological environment' as 'a nested arrangement of concentric structures, each contained within the next. These structures are referred to as micro, meso, exo and macro systems' (Bronfenbrenner, 1979, p. 2).

We have selected this approach as it captures many of the interactions between different systems victim-survivors are required to, directly or indirectly, navigate. Moreover, the model has successfully been applied in previous research on a VAWG system (see Adisa et al., 2020). We recognise that this implicit characterisation of system components as nested can be theorised alternatively as un-nested and in even more complex terms (Walby, 2003; Williams & Imam, 2007). For this chapter, we

---

[5] In the first phase, interviews were undertaken with 20 professionals—seven professionals implementing the project, four interviews with partner agency professionals, two staff members at the lead County, and with seven other relevant professionals and organisations not directly involved in implementing the intervention (included Police, and other DA orgs).

In the second phase, semi-structured interviews with 11 professionals representing a variety of specialisms and sectors. This included four professionals working within the local domestic abuse organisation responsible for delivering complex needs support, and seven professionals external to this organisation but who had either been instrumental in developing the original programme, or who regularly referred to the extended programme.

adopt this common nested ecological presentation to depict the multi-layered system structure while noting that *emergent* complex realities[6] experienced by migrant victim-survivors may lend itself to un-nested forms of systems structure, where systems do not overlap or follow a nested pattern.

We further apply Foster-Fishman's framework—an approach for conceptualising systems change—to re-examine the case study's system-oriented activities in relation to two aspects: assessing interactions and levers of change. We define this to mean those activities that involved 'sweeping in' of information from stakeholders and organisations that influenced intervention design and reshaping of relational elements in the system. This theoretical approach has since been accepted in examining systems change approaches in various comprehensive community settings since its development in 2007 (Foster-Fishman & Behrens, 2007; Foster-Fishman et al., 2007). A third aspect in the framework involves examining systems interdependencies which are a defining feature of complex systems, however, an in-depth discussion on complex systems is outside the scope of this chapter.

Migrant Victims-Survivors and Re-imagining Equitable Systems of Support

Figure 1 shows how a migrant survivor-centred ecosystem of support currently differs from those of their British-born peers affected by domestic abuse. We contend that nested ecological structures, social powers, and relationships shape migrants' experiences and have a role in re-designing any potential migrant survivor-centred system of support that is foregrounded in equity and effective coordination within communities that they live in, as against a complexity of need narrative which dominate the discourse on supporting migrant victims-survivors. Complexity ought not to be an excuse for systems limiting the thriving potential of victims-survivors. Reframing in systems change terms allows

---

[6] This notion of emergence is a characteristic of complex systems and relates to how the 'system as a whole cannot be reduced to the properties of constituent parts' (for a more thorough discussion on complexity and emergence, see Nicolis & Nicolis, 2012, p. 3).

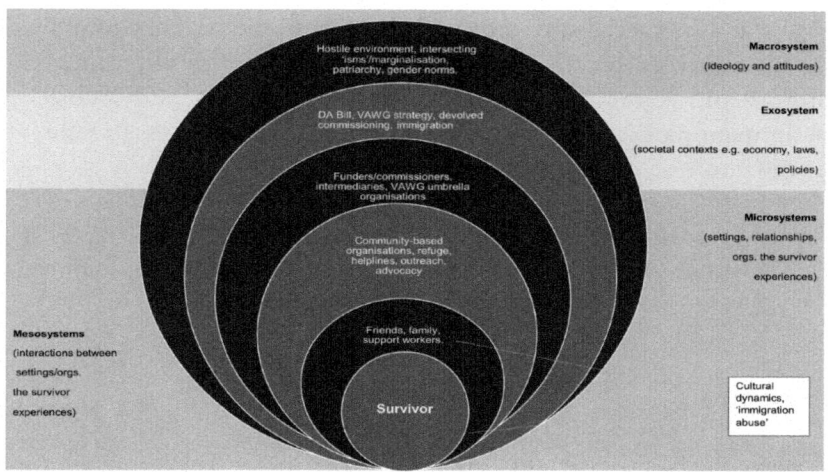

Fig. 1 Authors' nested system of support for migrant victims-survivors (Based on Bronfenbrenner [1979])

for a counter-discourse that is more empowering and focused on 'emancipation' (Midgley, 1996, p. 11).[7]

Migrant victim-survivors are situated within multiple interconnected settings, from broader policy landscapes to their relationships with their social support network, which interact to facilitate or hinder migrant victim-survivors access to support. This depiction is important and useful for two main reasons; (1) to help those who are designing interventions to have a greater appreciation of local systems change; and (2) to identify the key local system levers which matter for improving the outcomes for migrant victims-survivors in community-based settings.

Microsystem

An individual's microsystem encompasses the social settings, institutions, and relationships they directly experience and participate in; for example, a survivor's personal interactions with police, health, and social care

---

[7] In critical systems thinking terms this relates to 'improvement' which takes issues of power into consideration (see Midgley, 1996, p. 11).

services and/or specialist domestic abuse organisations. They found that migrant survivors directly engaging with mainstream services, including statutory and voluntary sector organisations, were frequently subject to discrimination or disadvantage. This included reduced access to resources due to (actual or perceived) immigration status:

> When I first turned to [refuge] for help two years ago, as an unemployed foreigner not entitled to benefits, I didn't receive any help. I was told that refuge is also classified as a benefit which I can't get.

Mesosystems

An individual's mesosystem can be defined in terms of interrelations between one or more social settings that a person has some direct contact or involvement with; for example, the interactions between a survivor's complex needs worker and their Immigration Advisor or social care services. Enhancing cross-sector and inter-professional relations can go some way towards mitigating the delays and challenges experienced by migrant survivors in relation to navigating the Hostile Environment.

Additionally, highly bureaucratic systems can influence interrelations within the system and extend to the type of language being used within the system. As one interviewee noted, given that many professionals navigate this changing policy/legal landscape with difficulty, it is likely to be more challenging for survivors:

> There's so much jargon, so many changes and updates, so many abbreviations and acronyms, it's really difficult to know. And it's not until you actually work in a particular area that you pick up some of those. I mean, I'm still having to scratch my head and think, 'Oh, what does that one mean?', almost on a daily basis. […] A lot of people just don't know what they're entitled to, and they're scared to ask just in case they they're already getting something that they shouldn't.

Macrosystems

The macrosystem refers to the social, economic, and cultural milieu that a person inhabits. Macrosystems are composed of laws and policies, economic systems, educational practices, prevailing ideologies, and cultural norms and the 'institutional structure[s] characteristic of a particular culture or subculture' (Bronfenbrenner, 1981, p. 9). Hostile Environment policies and austerity are examples of macrosystem-level contexts that are relevant to migrant survivors.

The NRPF labelling with respect to those with insecure immigration status led to a powerful financial disincentive around supporting survivors with, or believed to have, NRPF, particularly for smaller refugees locally. These was compounded by the fact that many professionals seem either to lack knowledge about the avenues that are open to survivors with NRPF, or lack faith that these options will be effective, remaining fearful about financial repercussions. As illustrated by one professional working locally:

> It's quite shameful that refuges around the country, as soon as they heard it was a foreign name, their next question was, "Has she got recourse?" And they were putting recourse to public funds ahead of safety, even when we had a guarantee from Children's Services or my team to underwrite the funding and the costs of that placement. And that continues to be a problem.

One key finding from our evaluation was that we observed a wariness among professionals that were involved in the intervention. One professional explained that this wariness was linked to the potential for prolonged and complex engagement *with the immigration and benefits system* when working with migrant survivors, with some survivors—and by extension the services supporting them—getting stuck in financial limbo for months waiting for these issues to get resolved:

> We took somebody in, oh probably 18 months ago and they're still in one of our buildings and we still haven't got their benefits sorted out. And we are still ordering a groceries delivery every week. What happens is the Department of Work and Pensions do a paper file for migrants

with NRPF, because they can't do electronic filing if they haven't got a National Insurance number. And if you've got NRPF, you don't have a National Insurance number.

Exosystem

A person's exosystem consists of one or more social settings that they have no direct contact or involvement with, but which affects their immediate context: for example, the interactions between domestic abuse support service staff, funders, and commissioners, or between domestic abuse support service staff and other organisations may indirectly impact a survivor who is accessing support through a particular service. A good example is the funding ecosystem issue. Adisa et al. (2020) found that funding shortages and short-term funding continue to limit the sustainability of support programmes, contribute to staff turnover and precarity and constrain services' ability to plan for, and invest in, the long-term.

As one professional interviewed as part of the evaluation noted, 'there are few certainties when it comes to funding; even with the introduction of a statutory duty for local authorities to provide DA (Domestic Abuse) accommodation, there was no '*guarantee from the [name of funder redacted] that funding would remain at the same or a higher level*'.

Given the possibility of year-on-year changes to local authority budgets, an authority could therefore '*double their accommodation one year then receive a reduced budget next year and have to substantially reduce provision*'. The lack of sustained, consistent funding—and the looming threat of a funding deficit when a grant comes to an end—can thereby disincentivise expanding and investing in services.

Translating Systems Thinking into Uncovering Community-based System Change Interactions and Levers

In this section, a crucial part of the systems thinking approach used here loosely draws on the idea of boundary critique in critical systems heuristics (Ulrich, 1996), that is understanding the boundary judgements and elements within the system in relation to the targeted issue. Building on Churchman's (1970) ideas for 'sweeping in information' for improvement, Ulrich put forward the theory of boundary critique as means for surfacing 'boundary judgements' regarding what is/is not relevant when designing solutions is a key component of systemic intervention and is intended to 'sweep in' marginalised viewpoints. Here in this chapter, the boundary concept is an important component for 'thinking in systems', and for improving comprehensiveness about system change, however, boundaries are often not absolute and rigidly defined (ibid).

System levers of change relate to the conditions and capacities for change (e.g. shared resources, policies, practices, relational dynamics, and so on), which can be linked to evidenced change efforts (Adisa et al., 2023).

Understanding the Boundaries and Perspectives within the System in Relation to the Targeted Issue

Human systems are typified by societal norms, and every human system is made up of people who are shaped by these societal norms, cultural, and individual circumstances (Vickers, 1983). These norms can shape and influence the way that systems of support are constructed, and who is constructing them.

For example, the Regional Wide Infrastructure Organisation (RWIC)[8] in our case study example, brought stakeholders together to co-design the intervention, which was then successfully funded. The Appendix (Table 1) depicts the types of organisations that were involved in this

---

[8] This has been anonymised and name changed.

process. We identified 15 key actors within our case study example. The system of actors and relationships[9] mentioned here does not depict all of the system components and elements (e.g. at post-bid success stage) and have been used here simply to provide an example of system interactions and to surface values and boundary judgements, during the bid development and pre-implementation stage. Infrastructure organisations like the RWIC can help build capacity in the sector, and can help facilitate systems convening to identify resourcing needs and solutions.

As mentioned earlier, in the two counties where the case study is located, issues were jointly identified by key stakeholders and the main issue was identified through a series of engagement and discussion meetings, about the additional pressures on local services who were having to support victims/survivors of domestic abuse with insecure immigration status. This meant that for this group of people, they would be ineligible for state benefits and therefore were unable to access conventional refuge beds. Refuge provision is a lifeline to victims fleeing abuse to ensure safety is a priority and to work out the pathways of support ad recovery for the individual (Allen et al., 2023).

These local multi-agency stakeholders identified a need to develop a clear pathway for all migrant victims/survivors of domestic abuse in the two counties. RWIC took careful steps in 'sweeping in' information from different stakeholders and developing this shared consensus in taking a co-created partnership approach.

The Community-Based System of Actors and Boundaries

One of the benefits of system thinking is that we were able to revisit these key actors and relationships retrospectively in a self-reflexive manner to identify the levers of change, as well as to reflect on our role as academics (who evaluated the intervention); and practitioners (who co-designed and implemented the intervention). For example, both our practitioner collaborators (Hill and Pack) felt that community outreach worked as

---

[9] This is not an exhaustive list as this does not include all the referring organisations, for example.

a system lever, and made a significant difference to the achieving of local systems change as evidenced through the evaluations, and this lever of engagement continues to shape their ongoing work in subsequent interventions design, for example in helping young people living and experiencing abuse in their homes, and who have disclosed the abuse to safeguarding teams in schools. It also offers an opportunity to identify and clarify emerging problems, particularly for migrant families. As both practitioners shared in their reflections during the writing of this chapter: 'The system currently creates fear for service when it comes to victims of domestic abuse identifying with NRPF; smaller agencies/refugees are scared of being out of pocket if they take an 'NRPF victim' into their accommodation, and can't move them on when the limited discretionary funding ends. They also worry about the additional costs. Safety needs to be prioritised first for victims, and not worries of being unable to access accommodation when fleeing abuse. We contacted many agencies with bedspaces, who refused to take our NRPF referral, even though we had the funding agreed. Also many refuges are tenancy agreements and with NRPF you are not entitled to hold a tenancy.' Additionally, the language of systems thinking can enhance the use of empowering descriptors in surfacing what change means to those involved in providing support to victims-survivors.

During the designing of the case study intervention (prior to the funding success stage), there was strong consensus on the problem statement and need identification—both empirically and normatively.

The facts selected demonstrated the great thought that went into identifying and clarifying the problem statement by multi-agencies at the initial meetings. The empirical observations and judgements made by those involved were clear and considered important by the loosely-defined informal 'consortium' involved in developing the proposal, and facilitated by the RWIC.

The following empirical selectivity of facts was used:

- Use of ONS (Office for National Statistics) Statistics (police force data) to demonstrate rise in DA incidents in both counties, migration profile of both counties. Case study accounts of the need and vulnerability of victims-survivors, provided by police officers responding to

DA incidents, including police officers having to pay for emergency accommodation from their own pockets in some cases.

- Use of information from existing service providers (VCSE (Voluntary, Community & Social Enterprises)) based on their caseloads about the unique needs of migrant victims-survivors, for example, through the literature, which has documented robustly, about the language barrier faced by migrant victim-survivors.
- Domestic Abuse Needs Assessment conducted by the Office of the Police and Crime Commissioner (OPCC) in the lead county emphasised the regional need for culturally responsive services, catering to the specific needs of migrant, Black and minoritised communities, Roma, Gypsy, and Traveller survivors, and particularly for survivors facing obstacles in accessing support in relation to NRPF status.

Through a boundary critique approach, one can examine the normative selectivity of values: here, beneficiaries in relation to those with insecure status, as well as the condition of being 'ordinarily resident' in either county. To underscore this point, we noted that powerful stories of need like Julia's were used to convincingly make the case for support, and there was a strong sense of feeling of injustice across all the agencies present that this gap needed to addressed.

However, the duration of the short-term accommodation provision within the intervention as set out by the counties was incompatible with the normative views held by the VCSEs (Voluntary, Community & Social Enterprises) who argued that safe emergency housing for migrant victims and survivors needed to be longer because of the 'hostile' bureaucratic immigration systems that they are navigating. Our evaluation findings have since corroborated the VCSE's viewpoints to be correct. The lead implementing organisation had to find innovative ways to extend the accommodation using different creative funding resources from elsewhere. Pack and Hill have reflected that: 'Ideally, the victim of abuse should be entitled to 12 months of support/accommodation to enable them to access immigration options advice and follow the advice, and to work, if appropriate. Also, to support the prosecution of the abuser and have justice for their experiences. Currently, it is difficult to support a prosecution if you have had to return to your country of origin, and abusers will tell victims they are not going to be prosecuted and taken seriously. This allows the abuse to continue and word to spread amongst migrant victims that support is not accessible'.

Additionally, following the bid success, the evaluation team observed divergent 'perspectives' with respect to the following aspects. These aspects included:

- Why only one of the selected counties was assigned the lead and responsibility for the intervention, contrary to the multi-agency partnership approach developed during the intervention design stage.
- How decisions were made with respect to the selection of delivery partners/organisations.
- Model of delivery of the intervention that was chosen.
- Bureaucratic communication and language that was being used, which seemed incompatible with the inclusive and transparent 'co-production' language that was used at the start.

In our reflections, we opine that while those responsible for administering the funds received at the county level may have embarked on a process that was deemed to be more 'efficient', this approach to systems improvement interacts with that of power imbalances, and those who hold most power, as characterised by control of system resources.

System Resources (Funding and Commissioning)

It is imperative to briefly reflect on resource flows, and how these flows shape system behaviour and structure (Adisa et al., 2020). To do so, we reflect on how structures of power manifest within and across systems and actors which provide resources (e.g. funders) and those who seek access to them (e.g. community-based support organisations, service providers).

One unintended consequence of this power imbalance is that certain interests or problems are given legitimacy over others. In future inquiry, an individual or organisational lens could be adopted here (i.e. reflecting on the interactions of systems of oppression and limited access to resources available to those supporting migrant victim-survivors), and this inquiry does deserve attention. However due to brevity, we focus instead on a collective—or relational systems—approach to power, in line with the ecological model and systems change approach proposed earlier in this chapter.

One system change lever identified through this retrospective reflection of systems change properties was the intentional approach to community engagement in intervention design, which followed a cocreation process during the bid development process, which 2 out of the 4 authors were privy to (Adisa and Hill). The scaled-back partnership approach (lead contractor and subcontracting organisation) arrived at was driven by a competitive tendering process, which differed from the more expansive collaborative approach (described by one participant as a 'Consortium approach comprising of multi-agencies') suggested during the codesign of the intervention. We retrospectively examined the bid document to uncover the types of actors (Table 1), and interactions, and the boundary judgements specifically at the intervention design stage.

To understand such influence, we characterise the notion of power as resources/money. Here, we view power (resource sharing) as mutable and potentially negotiable. The way power is shared within the community-based system can impact organisations' sustainability, services delivered, and support for victim-survivors. Power structures at the macro, exo, and mesosystem levels manifest at the microsystem level. Those with power shape and structure the environment in which migrant victim-survivors are placed and which they are forced to navigate. The issue of border control takes place over the protection of those potentially victimised. This characteristic of collectively owned and shared notion of power is interesting in the sense that it can be understood as a condition for systems change, and it challenges simplistic binary connotations of power (e.g. the powerful versus the powerless, to one of being unequally dispersed across levels and groups). Development and social change scholars have well-utilised ideas of power over the years for systems change improvement. One good example is John Gaventa's power cube, which is characterised by dimensions and subcomponents of power represented by forms, spaces, and levels to depict a set of dynamic interrelationships in relation to participation and engagement at a local, national, and global level. It has become a thinking tool for using concepts such as invisible power and created spaces to explore power issues in social change settings (Gaventa, 2021).

The political discourses, as we have described above, but equally the current dysfunctional nature and structure of funding systems continue to erode the use of collective systems of power to improve coordination and collaboration at the community-level (Adisa et al., 2020). For instance, the bidding system in place has resulted in many community-based specialist services competing for money with larger generalist organisations (despite compelling research showing the importance of specialist services in supporting those experiencing domestic abuse, for example, see Harris and Hodges, 2019).

Funding structures can therefore perpetuate the oppressive systems—those at the edge become further marginalised due to limited support systems available (Adisa et al., 2020). Similarly, austerity policies and subsequent funding cuts lead to the increasing withdrawal of support to certain public services, which affect women (Pearson, 2019). These examples illustrate how power exercised at these levels—within macro, exo, and mesosystems—determines the power that actors are granted within microsystems.

Notably, while the evaluation we undertook found that the specialist DA service provider delivered high-quality services, and the cost–benefit analysis identified significant savings because of the project, the funding for the project was not continued after the original funding period, which may not come as a surprise to many working in the sector. Compounded by the systemic issue of a bureaucratic hostile immigration system (a form of administrative violence, to use Dean Spade's term, see Spade, 2015), migrant-specific services in England and Wales are usually subjected to short-term and project-based funding which hinders their ability to provide consistent and sustainable support, leading to truncated pathways of support (DAC, 2021; 2022a, b) and system change efforts that are not reflective of a re-imagined vision of a sustainable emergent environment within which systems of support ought to operate within or be related to.

Summary, Recommendations, and Conclusion

We began with the story of Julia, a victim-survivor, and a summary of the literature to present these systemic issues faced by migrant victims-survivors. We also used a critical systems thinking lens to depict the multi-level system characteristics, which was then visually framed within an ecological framework. The key systemic issues that continue to influence systems of support for migrant victims and survivors include macrosystem factors such as national domestic abuse policies, the legacies of hostile environment policies, austerity, and political concepts such as 'illegality' and no recourse to public funds; exosystem factors such as the VAWG funding ecosystem, and intra-organisational and mesosystem influences such as financial risk aversion and underinvestment.

Short-term and project-focused funding within the VAWG sector contributes to a sense of precarity among service providers, disincentivising (potentially costly) engagement with service users who have, or are believed to have, NRPF, and reducing services' ability to invest in developing specialist provision. A shift to longer-term, sustainable funding for crucial VAWG services would ameliorate these barriers, thereby promoting more equitable provision of services and support for migrant victim-survivors. There is a need to use systems thinking to bring about long-term sustained change through an equitable, coordinated response right from the co-design of interventions, to the smarter commissioning processes.

Through reflective retrospective discussions, systems levers were identified which mitigated the impact of these system dysfunctionalities: transparent bidding process, equitable sharing of resources, and community outreach (to promote understanding, reach, and to build relationships). These levers of change have been shown to make a difference individually. Local systems change efforts should have at its core equity-oriented practice, and a commitment to build awareness of the flattening of hierarchies of power in collaborative and coordinated community endeavours.

Place-based attributes can also create emergent properties (such as locally embedded complexities) in the system which can make it challenging to coordinate systems change efforts, but also offer up emergent opportunities for collaboration and coordination. As an example, in the local context of our case study, short-term emergency accommodation was provided to single victim-survivors without children (a gap identified through data and insights earlier surfaced through boundary critique), which was an innovative feature of the intervention, to mitigate some of the well-known issues of 'postcode lottery' in relation to service availability and provision, which we do not have space to discuss in detail here.

It is important then for local systems change approaches to note that community-based responses can be impacted by geographical size of counties. Smaller counties might necessitate victim-survivor journeys across local authority boundaries for safety and privacy reasons when fleeing domestic abuse situations. Domestic abuse is known to be the cause of significant 'internal migration' between counties, with around 10,000 recorded journeys across local authority boundaries to access DA services between 2008 and 2009 (Bowstead, 2015, p. 335). Fast to forward to present day, these recorded journeys are likely to be significantly greater.

We recognise that in some areas, refuges and other forms of DA provision are often not local but national services, which have implications for mobility and 'flow' between counties, and which a static nested representation (based on the ecological framework used in this chapter) is limited in depicting interactions in dynamic terms across time and space, adding layers of complexity to the picture. Uncovering and depicting these system interdependencies are a matter of further theorising work on complex systems thinking.

Finally, in this chapter, we have demonstrated how critical systems thinking ideas (in practical terms) can signify and enhance systems change. Considering the migration context, the role of global actors may be significant. Therefore, there is scope for a greater appreciation of the interconnectedness of the *local, national and global* aspects of systems of support that interface with the mobilities and securitisation of migrant victims-survivors (see Innes, 2023). Additionally, there is an opportunity for more exploration (particularly in drawing on complexity concepts) in understanding and identifying the interdependencies in systems of support, and specifically to explore emergent spaces for change between multiple systems and subsystems (as shown here), which help to improve the inequitable systems of support that migrant victims-survivors are expected to navigate to get support and help.

Appendix

See Table 1.

Table 1 Key actors and relationships attributable to the case study systemic intervention

Name	Type of organisation/role
County1	County 1
County2	County 2
CharityC	Lead contractor charity
CharitySC	Subcontractor charity
Charity P1	Charity stakeholder—external to the intervention
Charity P2	Charity stakeholder—external to the intervention
Charity P3	Charity stakeholder—external to the intervention
Charity P4	Charity stakeholder—external to the intervention
Charity P5	Charity stakeholder—external to the intervention
Charity P6	Charity stakeholder—external to the intervention
Charity P7	Charity stakeholder—external to the intervention
PoliceC1	Statutory stakeholder—external to the intervention
PoliceC2	Statutory stakeholder—external to the intervention
University	Evaluation, and facilitated co-produced public engagement event
RWIC[a]	Infrastructure organisation

Note [a]Region-wide infrastructure org

References

Adisa O. (2019). *The effectiveness of interventions supporting migrant victims/ survivors of domestic abuse: An evidence brief*. University of Suffolk

Adisa, O., Allen, K., Kumari, M., Weir, R., & Bond, E. (2020). *Mapping the VAWG funding ecosystem in England and Wales*. Project Report. Centre for Abuse Research. SISER (Suffolk Institute for Social and Economic Research).

Adisa, O., Allen, K., Manning, M., Ferreira, J., & Horvath, M. (2023). Drive systems change evaluation: Final report. *Institute for Social Justice and Crime*. University of Suffolk

Allen, K., Adisa, O., & Hermolle, M. (2023). Redefining safety: A narrative review of literature on the underground and open or 'Dutch'models of refuge. *Journal of Gender-Based Violence, 7*(3), 483–498.

Anitha, S. (2010). No recourse, no support: State policy and practice towards South Asian women facing domestic violence in the UK. *British Journal of Social Work, 40*, 462–479.

Azmanova, A. (2018). Relational, structural and systemic forms of power: The 'right to justification' confronting three types of domination. *Journal of Political Power, 11*(1), 68–78.

Bowstead, J. C. (2015). Why women's domestic violence refuges are not local services. *Critical Social Policy, 35*(3), 327–349.

Bronfenbrenner, U. (1979). *The ecology of human development*. Harvard University Press.

Bronfenbrenner, U. (1981). *The ecology of human development: Experiments by nature and design*. Harvard University Press. ProQuest Ebook Central. https://ebookcentral-proquest-com.uos.idm.oclc.org/lib/ucsl/detail.action?docID=3300702. Accessed 25 July 2021.

Churchman, C. W. (1970). Operations research as a profession. *Management Science, 17*(2), B–37.

Clarke, A., & Crane, A. (2018). Cross-sector partnerships for systemic change: Systematized literature review and agenda for further research. *Journal of Business Ethics, 150*(2), 303–313.

Domestic Abuse Commissioner. (2021). *Safety before Status: Improving pathways to support for migrant victims of domestic abuse*. https://domesticabusecommissioner.uk/wp-content/uploads/2021/10/Safety-Before-Status-Report-2021.pdf

Domestic Abuse Commissioner. (2022a). *A patchwork of provision—Technical report.* https://domesticabusecommissioner.uk/wp-content/uploads/2022/11/A-Patchwork-of-Provision_Technical-Report_Nov-2022_Final.pdf

Domestic Abuse Commissioner. (2022b). *A patchwork of provision: How to meet the needs of victims and survivors across England and Wales.* https://assets.publishing.service.gov.uk/government/uploads/system/uploads/attachment_data/file/1120642/E02828098_A_Patchwork_of_Provision_Accessible.pdf

Erez, E., Adelman, M., & Gregory, C. (2009). Intersections of immigration and domestic violence: Voices of battered immigrant women. *Feminist Criminology, 4*, 32–56.

Ferreira, J. (2021). Migrant women victims of intimate partner violence and the criminal justice system in Portugal. *Journal of Interpersonal Violence, 36*(13–14). NP6767-NP6802.

Foster-Fishman, P. G., Nowell, B., & Yang, H. (2007). Putting the system back into systems change: A framework for understanding and changing organizational and community systems. *American Journal of Community Psychology, 39*(3), 197–215. https://doi.org/10.1007/s10464-007-9109-0

Foster-Fishman, P. G., & Behrens, T. R. (2007). Systems change reborn: Rethinking our theories, methods, and efforts in human services reform and community-based change. *American Journal of Community Psychology, 39*(3), 191–196.

France, A., Bottrell, D., & Armstrong, D. (2012). *A theory of the political ecology of youth and crime. Em a political ecology of youth and crime.* London: Palgrave Macmillan.

Gaventa, J. (2021). Linking the prepositions: Using power analysis to inform strategies for social action. *Essays on Evolutions in the Study of Political Power*, 109–130.

Ham, C., & Alderwick, H. (2015). *Place-based systems of care: A way forward for the NHS in England.* https://www.kingsfund.org.uk/sites/default/files/field/field_publication_file/Place-based-systems-of-care-Kings-Fund-Nov-2015_0.pdf. Accessed 25 July 2021.

Harris, L., & Hodges, K. (2019). Responding to complexity: Improving service provision for survivors of domestic abuse with 'complex needs'. *Journal of gender-based violence, 3*(2), 167–184.

Innes, A. (2023). Migration, vulnerability, and experiences of insecurity: Conceptualising insecure migration status. *Social Sciences, 12*(10), 540.

Midgley, G. (1996). What is this thing called CST? *Critical Systems Thinking: Current Research and Practice*, 11–24.

Midgley, G. (2001). *Systemic intervention: Philosophy, methodology, and practice.* Springer Science & Business Media.

Menjívar, C., & Salcido, O. (2002). Immigrant women and domestic violence: Common experiences in different countries. *Gender & Society, 16*, 898–920.

Nicolis, G., & Nicolis, C. (2012). *Foundations of complex systems: Emergence, information and predicition.* World Scientific.

Orloff, L., & Garcia, O. (2013). Dynamics of domestic violence experienced by immigrant victims1 2.

Pearson, R. (2019). A feminist analysis of neoliberalism and austerity policies in the UK. *Soundings, 71*(71), 28–39.

Rittel, H. W., & Webber, M. M. (1973). Dilemmas in a general theory of planning. *Policy Sciences, 4*(2), 155–169.

Raj, A., & Silverman, J. (2002). Violence against immigrant women: The roles of culture, context, and legal immigrant status on intimate partner violence. *Violence against Women, 8*, 637–398.

Salcido, O., & Adelman, M. (2004). 'He has me tied with the blessed and damned papers': Undocumented immigrant battered women in Phoenix, Arizona. *Human Organization, 63*(2), 162–173.

Spade, D. (2015). *Normal life: Administrative violence, critical trans politics, and the limits of law.* Duke University Press.

Vickers, G. (1983). *Human systems are different.* Harper & Row.

Walby, S. (2003, April). *Complexity theory, globalisation and diversity. In conference of the British Sociological Association.* University of York.

Williams, B., & Imam, I. (2007). *Systems concepts in evaluation: An expert anthology.* EdgePress of Inverness.

Worrall, R., & Leech, D. (2018). Will place-based leadership be the right remedy for health and social care? *British Journal of Healthcare Management, 24*(2), 9094.

Tools and Conceptual Ideas
for Engendering Systems Thinking

A Socio-Technical Approach to Researching Technologically Facilitated Intimate Abuse

Carolyn Leader

Introduction

Globally, the use of technological objects to mediate intimate partner abuse is becoming increasingly common, with Refuge in 2020 demonstrating that 72% of referrals to their services included a form of technological-mediated abuse (Christie & Wright, 2020; Kellam, 2020). The use of technological objects is arguably challenging and blurring the boundaries and traditional dualisms between public and private, structure and agency, and human and non-human, with Hutchby and Moran-Ellis (2001, p. 3) suggesting "the significance of technologies lies not in what an artefact is, not in what it specifically does, but in what it enables or affords as it mediates the relationship between its user and other individuals". Therefore, technological objects should not be considered fixed entities but mediated through the user interface as fluid and flexible objects dependent on the user and embedded in the

C. Leader (✉)
University of Suffolk, Ipswich, UK
e-mail: c.leader2@uos.ac.uk

© The Author(s), under exclusive license to Springer Nature
Switzerland AG 2024
O. Adisa and E. Bond (eds.), *Tackling Domestic Abuse and Sexual Violence*, Palgrave
Studies in Victims and Victimology, https://doi.org/10.1007/978-3-031-58600-2_4

contemporary human condition (Berg, 1999; Bond, 2014; Mackenzie & Wajcman, 1999). Considering this, throughout this chapter, I will utilise the phrase 'technology-mediated intimate partner abuse' to shed light on the growing impact technology has on abuse in intimate relationships. Rather than drawing on the more traditional language of domestic abuse and domestic violence, I have made the conscious decision to reframe domestic abuse/violence within the remits of 'intimate partner' to transition the language from historical conceptualisations in an attempt to recognise how abuse does transpire in any form of intimate relationship, irrespective of sexual orientation, gender or relationship status.

The advancements in information communication and technology in the twenty-first century have triggered an exponential change in how humans communicate and operationalise their lives, mediated by technological devices and applications. Accordingly, Mackenzie and Wajcman (1999) note how homes are increasingly becoming infused within a web of digital networks and technologies, challenging the boundaries between technology and privacy (Shapiro, 1998). With Myerson (2001, p. 9) utilising the development of the telephone as an example, "The phone is an object and a technology. But it is also part of a system of ideas, even a way of life. The phone has become part of an idea of the family, of intimacy and work". Myerson (2001, p. 9) presents an essential construct of the relationship between technology and the self; building on the aspect of the telephone within technology-mediated abuse, we can potentially reshape and theorise the notion by drawing on semiotics and the work of Barthes's (1957) and ideas located within connotation and denotation, to researching technology-mediated abuse and how perpetrators, victim/survivors, researchers, policymakers come to understand technological objects. Considering this application concerning technological objects, the denotation of the technological object acts as a sign, thus providing the literal definition/designed purpose of the digital and/or technological objects. However, when we start to consider the connotations of the digital and/or technological objects, this begins to allow us to consider the subjective meanings of technological abuses and alternative worldviews that can be applied to the object, allowing for othered meaning beyond the intentional. Accordingly, applying and considering this through the lens of 'tech abuse' can be considered as redefining and configuring the mechanisms, meanings, and possibilities located within technological objects from the literal to embodied meanings of abuse. They are drawing on our previous example of the telephone, potentially changing and challenging it as a mechanism of communication between family and friends, which elicits feelings of comfort and safety, to an object of anxiety, fear, safety, and harm. Within abuse research, it is imperative to consider both the denotations and connotations of digital objects and the stories they can elicit.

Coincidingly, it becomes imperative to recognise the rise of digital network society, as proposed by Castells (1996, 1997, 2000). For Castells (2000), technological advancements should be taken seriously, for many of the ideas located in network society are relatable to current society, with Castells (2004, p. 3) defining network society as "a society whose social structure is made of networks powered by microelectronics-based information and communication technologies". Utilising the network society to begin our understanding of technology-mediated intimate partner abuse, two specific features should be noted: 'space and flows' and 'timeless time'. Castell (2004) notes how these two concepts do not reconfigure the meanings of space and time but now operate in co-existence within them alongside being cultural expressions of a network society. Moreover, the concepts of space and time still exist, but the associated limitations and boundaries of space and time are becoming less evident. Therefore, the combination of the network society combined with the reconfiguration of space and time can now transition to technology-mediated intimate abuse, becoming a timeless and spaceless phenomenon that has now arguably redefined the geographical, spatial and time boundaries of abuse for both the victim/ survivor and perpetrator (Castells, 2000; Hang et al., 2009). From this, it is, therefore, arguable that the spaceless and timeless boundaries of technology-mediated intimate abuse transitions perpetrators to an omnipresent within the victim/survivor's life, often inescapable through the ever-emerging and advancing technological devices and applications (George & Harris, 2014; Harris, 2018). Therefore, this reconfiguration of digital intimacies and digital lives with the intersection of technology requires researchers, stakeholders and policymakers to consider new knowledge constructions and theorisations into the role and relationship between the self, technology, digital networks, and online spaces and places, which have and are challenging the formation, maintenance, and values of relationship 'norms' alongside acceptable and non-acceptable digital technological behaviours and intrusions in daily life, transitioning to abuse which this chapter aims to explore (Hess, 2015).

In this introduction, we have briefly explored the relationship between technological objects and intimate partner abuse to set the foundation for the rest of the chapter. The chapter adopts a position of theoretical and discipline plurality, drawing from theories and disciplines such as systems theory, actor-network theory, socio-technical studies, and sociology in consideration of researching technologically mediated intimate partner abuse. Defining technological objects and technological-mediated abuse can be challenging due to the subjective nature of the relationship of each component. In particular, this chapter acknowledges and responds to Schwarz's (2021) focus on the changing ontological status of networks, emphasising the need for new ways of thinking and theorisations underpinning the plurality of our analysis. The focus of the chapter moving forward is on technology-mediated intimate abuse, also known as 'Tech Abuse'. It draws knowledge from the field of the Internet of Things (IoT) to help guide our understanding of digital and technological objects. The IoT encompasses networks, services, and internet-connected smart technologies such as laptops, smart watches, mobile phones, security systems, and home assistance. It is located within the IoT; technologies have become tools for perpetrators to monitor, shame, harass, stalk, intimidate, and threaten their victims, leading to the rise of technology-mediated intimate abuse. The structure of the chapter will be developed through two sections; the first section will focus on considerations when researching technology-mediated intimate partner abuse, drawing on the main theoretical paradigms of this chapter, systems thinking and actor-network theory, demonstrating their theoretical orientations and how they can be applied to 'tech abuse' research. The second section develops on the arguments located within the first half of this chapter to consider the application of systems thinking to one of the main challenges in abuse research before concluding the literature presented.

Researching Technologically Mediated Intimate Partner Abuse and Theoretical Frameworks

Notably, violence and abuse in any form as an area of research can be highly problematic and challenging phenomena to operationalise and conceptualise, crossing multiple layers of the social ecology (individual, family, social, and community). The ideas and constructions of what is considered acceptable or unacceptable behaviours and what can be constituted as harm or abuse are often culturally influenced and constantly under revision as society and cultural norms evolve globally, thus transitioning intimate partner abuse to one of the most sensitive, challenging, and political areas to research (Fraga, 2016). Similar to other areas of research, abuse research aims to elicit change within society through stakeholders, policy, and government. However, these all too often fall foul of similar pitfalls in other research areas when implementing change. Stroh (2015) indicates how a phenomenon's underlying problem(s) are too often not fully understood, with symptoms becoming the focal point of change, often creating short-term success but mediating long-term resolutions, which can produce unintentional adverse outcomes. When considered through the lens of research into the remit of technologically mediated intimate partner abuse, this could result in perpetrators learning new tactics of technologically mediated abuse or finding systematic loopholes that can be exploited to the detriment of their victim. According to Christie and Wright (2020), research into technology mediating indicates how services that respond to 'tech abuse' often lack training awareness and technical knowledge to respond adequately. A potential and essential component to respond to Stroh's (2015) claims is through the lens of system-thinking and actor-network theory. System thinking, as a tool for social change, is helping to change the landscape of how 'problems/solutions' are to be considered and is paving the way forward to help influence stakeholders, policy-makers, researchers, and governments to understand the often complex and discursive issues prevalent in society today and the roles they play individually and collectively in seeking successfully long-term change and solutions. The proceeding section outlines the main theoretical paradigms when researching technology-mediated abuse.

Theoretical Paradigms

Systems Thinking

Adopting a system-thinking approach to researching technology-mediated intimate partner abuse requires understanding what a system is. Meadows (2008, p. 2) defines a system as a "set of things – people, cells, molecules, or whatever – interconnected in such a way that they produce their own pattern of behaviour over time". According to Meadows (2008), a system has a function and purpose, built on interconnections and elements with the purpose of the system relatable to behaviour(s) and with systems designed to achieve and uphold what they currently do (Carne et al., 2019; Meadows, 2008: Stroh, 2015). In systems thinking, systems are considered broadly, including but not limited to behaviour(s), policies, people, socio-cultural drivers, and structural inequalities that can impact the occurrence, prevention, and responses. In essence, system thinking aims to understand the common factors within a problem/issue and seeks to understand how they are connected within and between the system working as a complex whole. Acknowledging how a system is made up of interrelated components in addition to the relationship between the components is a two-pronged approach. System thinking requires the recognition and understanding of the importance of the relationship between the components in understanding the behaviour(s) within a system in addition to the individual components. System thinkers Meadows (2008) and Stroh (2015) emphasise the importance of learning the individual components of a system but also place a great emphasis on the need to understand how the system operates as a whole, drawing on the notion of how a system can be greater than the sum of its parts. This becomes vital when researching and analysing systems such as those examining technology-mediated intimate partner abuse or, as Rittel and

Webber (1973) define it, the 'wicked problem' due to the multiple inter-acting components that change over time and space when planning any social policy problem (Carne et al., 2019). To further the difficulty, 'wicked problems' are considered as having no one correct answer, with multi-stakeholders holding and adopting differing priorities, language, understandings, norms, and viewpoints. Kaplan et al. (2017) draw atten-tion to the fact that many stakeholders and professionals often work in silos when considering 'wicked problems', resulting in stakeholders and professionals often not having the language, knowledge(s), or tools to bring everything together as a whole, which is where system thinking responds to bridge this gap (Carne et al., 2019).

Moreover, for this chapter, system thinking will be considered at its most basic level, which requires all actors and players (stakeholders, poli-cymakers, researchers, etc.) to become self-accountable and responsible for their part in the 'problem' they wish to solve; by doing so, they can influence the system where they have the most control: themselves. This means that players and actors in the system must first understand their role, including how they can affect change but also how they may contribute to the problem unintentionally. As the actors and players in the system gain a better understanding of their position and posi-tion in line with others in the system, they can better understand how they may have been creating unsatisfactory results or become fixed in a particular solution-focused symptomatic response, missing the bigger picture or root cause of the issue. It is only then when the actors and players within the system have analysed their own position that they can begin to appreciate and understand the viewpoints, stances, motiva-tions, strengths, and weaknesses of others within the system and can start working together to develop a system map and approach to the problem. In this manner, system thinking allows for the building of networks between key stakeholders and researchers, for example, leading to the development of a more diverse perspective and deeper understanding of the phenomena from several perspectives, with each player under-standing their contribution. This kaleidoscopic view can arguably allow for more profound reflections of the problem and help uncover blind spots in thinking, leading to a deeper understanding of the purpose the system is accomplishing. In support, Stroh (2015) suggests that when addressing complex problems with a singular worldview, root causes often remain masked due to overt and explicit symptomatic responses and linear thinking.

Accordingly, the brief overview of systems thinking here introduces researchers to other ways of thinking about technology-mediated intimate partner abuse; the proceeding section will position actor-network theory as a theoretical lens that seeks to understand the relationship of technology to society within a system-thinking approach. Firstly, the central tenets of actor-network theory will be discussed within the remit of technologically mediated intimate partner abuse before applying system-thinking and actor-network theory to two main concerns within research: language and communication.

Actor-Network Theory

From the outset, it should be noted that scholars such as Callen and Latour (1981), Law (1997), Latour (2000), and Inglis and Thorpe (2019) argue that actor-network theory is not a theory in the traditional sense but rather more a method to analyse actors (human and non-human: technological objects). Law (2003, p. 381) outlines the core principles of actor-network theory as "a central concern with the operations of power, the social conceived as a heterogeneous network, with knowledge action and power explained, as network effects embodied in the material forms". As previously drawn on with examples of connotation and denotation, the actor-network theory uses the metaphorical and literal realities to the applications of technology objects and networks, which can help a system-thinking approach to research. For example, Latour (1998) uses the illustration of a person's relationship with their electrical supplier; when applying the lens of actor-network theory, this would consider the person's relationship with the provider: through ideas of loyalty, fear of change but also the material objects (wires, copper, meters, energy) which provide the supply.

Taking this a step further to applying technologically mediated intimate partner abuse, Latour (1999) proposes how technological devices and objects can mediate in four senses. Firstly, technologies can create new possibilities and programmes for Latour (1999); the possibilities of transformation here can be located between the human and digital object: "You are a different person with a gun in your hand" (Latour, 1999, p. 179). Second, technologies allow for transforming and distributing new practices, associations and compositions, and exchanging performances. If, for one moment, we are to consider the performances of the self and technology in technology-mediated intimate partner abuse, a dramaturgical lens can help researchers to consider the backstage arena of both the self and technology linked to the 'problem' area systems thinking seeks to explore and expose for change to occur. Thirdly, technologies now afford time and space to be compressed, as noted previously by Castell within the network society.

Moreover, technologies can delegate and complete the work humans would have traditionally done, meaning humans no longer need to be present. The final point here is particularly pertinent when considering technology-mediated intimate partner abuse and the theoretical pluralism of this chapter. Building on this, the work of Foucault (1975) considers how discipline and punishment are a form of power that is not embodied but becomes a 'technology of power' aiming to make the human condition more controllable and manageable. For Foucault, he believed one does not have discipline or power. However, discipline and power become something a person does, with discipline becoming a set of practices and techniques forming a system. In this sense, discipline transforms the human condition into an obedient and docile body that is unique and independent but controlled.

Moreover, Foucault saw power not as oppressive but as a productive entity that has come to permeate the most intimate parts of human existence. These mechanisms of discipline and punishment in society are the foundation of Bentham's ideas of the panopticon. The panopticon can be considered a classic example of how technological objects and devices have now mediated intimate relationships exhibiting abusive and controlling tendencies, with the victim/survivor never knowing if they are being watched or monitored by the perpetrator, resulting in the victim/survivor acting as if they are being watched and monitored at all times with the victim/survivor acting as their own guard keeping them in place. Developing on this, Schwarz (2021) notes how technological objects and devices now allow users to monitor others' actions but not necessarily the monitoring exposing the transactional element of the network.

In summary, the pluralistic lens of actor-network theory applied here provides a way to begin conceptualising and locating technologically mediated abuse and understanding the role of digital objects in society today and how they operate on differing levels from the literal to the metaphorical. Therefore, it considers technological objects' explicit and implicit role in mediating abuse. The proceeding section will now consider our theoretical paradigms in line with Kaplan et al.'s (2017) Point of contention in research of 'wicked problems': language and communication.

The Role and Possibilities of Language and Definitions in Technologically Mediated Intimate Partner Abuse

As a starting point for researchers aiming to examine technology-mediated intimate partner abuse within the UK, understanding the challenges located in the semantics of language, as reflected in Kaplan et al. (2017) claims regarding language, it is therefore imperative to consider this within the remit of systems thinking and actor-network theory. The first point of contention arises when we consider how intimate partner abuse and technology-mediated abuse currently have no statutory definition within the UK. However, it is imperative to note how the implementation of the Domestic Abuse Act (2021) now provides a definition of domestic abuse but currently does not provide any explicit mention of the role of technology in intimate partner abuse with a range of strategies, policies and frameworks (cyber security policy, online harms policy, Domestic Abuse Act [2012]) dealing with the differing tenants of technology-mediated intimate partner abuse.

Recognising the multiple policies, stakeholders, and laws considering intimate partner abuse transitions to a requirement for a more explicit paradigm of knowledge and understanding. Therefore, it needs to be recognised that the current lack of consensus on language, definition, and application is a globalised phenomenon with no universally agreed definition of intimate partner abuse, domestic violence, or gender-based abuse or violence. The trajectory of conflicting definitions and terms for intimate partner abuse/violence, domestic abuse/violence, spousal violence, and family violence has often guided researchers to question what is at the core of these terms, who is and is not involved, the role of technology, in addition to questioning what constitutes violence and/ or abuse in an intimate relationship mediated by technology. Accordingly, the lack of consistent global application and definition has been argued by several scholars (Bachman, 2000; Bender, 2017; Burgess-Proctor, 2015; Fraga, 2016; Mirrlees-Black, 1995, 1999) to minimise victim/survivor understanding(s) and perceptions(s) of what constitutes technological-mediated abusive behaviours leading to many victim/survivors and perpetrators as not perceiving the behaviour(s) as abusive but a normal part of life/dating discourse.

In reflection of the first point of contention, we will now adopt a system-thinking perspective to this 'problem'. The adoption of a system-thinking response here requires researchers, stakeholders, and policymakers to recognise knowledge production as subjective, discursive, and continuous, placing methodological value within the ontological and epistemological standpoints of abuse, victim, perpetrator, and technology contingent on the discursive truths, subjective truths, and individually constructed and reconstructed performances of the self and technology in society (Gomm, 2008). This methodological reframing of technology-mediated intimate partner abuse combined with systems thinking acknowledges Stroth's (2015) point that eliciting change in any complex system requires continuous learning and recognising that knowledge is never fixed, static or complete but evolves over time, space, and place. Building on this, Matthewman (2011) has argued for a theoretical plurality when examining technologies as they can never truly be understood as dualisms of online, offline, and virtual, real world, literal, and metaphorical but constructed in a manner that compresses time and space, and public and private and affect the embodied and lived realities of its users. Accordingly, systems thinking draws on data collection from qualitative and quantitative philosophical traditions, with a marked emphasis on unveiling the intended and unintended outcomes of the research to monitor and explore any application of systemic theories of change (Stroth, 2015).

Recognising the semantics, understanding(s) and construction(s) of technology-mediated intimate partner abuse is the starting point for change within system thinking and for researchers to explicitly consider the semantics and definitions within their own fields and how this may affect participants' understandings, narratives, research impact, and outcomes. Developing a system-thinking approach in this manner requires the network (victim/survivor, perpetrator, researchers, policy-makers, governments, to name but a few) to develop a shared common agenda, including but not limited to a common language for communication and understanding separately and together why technology-mediated abuse and intimate partner abuse still persists in society today, considering substantial policy and legislative changes in an attempt to combat it in recent years. Utilising this shared language within and between the networks but also in consideration of abuse and technology more broadly can transition to a better understanding of how each part of the system is connected, often in non-obvious ways, but also creates an agenda for each part of the system to reflect on how they are contributing to the problem which in turn is affecting other parts. A key point within these considerations when researching technology-mediated intimate partner abuse is what Ling (2012) refers to as the 'taken-for-grantedness' of technologies that technological objects have now become so embedded in our daily lives that they are taken for granted in understanding and usage. Developing on this idea further, Kline and Pinch (1999) have examined technology through a social constructionist lens, arguing how technology and technological objects should be understood as offering different meanings within and between different social groups for differing purposes. This understanding requires interpretive flexibility of technological objects, user, and embodied self, recognising the many different meanings that can be applied to technology objects depending on social groups, societal norms, and user preferences (Bond, 2014). Kline and Pinch (1999), Ling's (2012), and Bond's (2014) considerations are a crucial component in a systems thinking approach whereby commonly taken-for-granted understandings are utilised to understand the problem rather than considerations into possible new root causes or other ways of knowing and understanding technology-mediated intimate partner abuse, reiterating the point that dominant rhetoric should be challenged and viewed within the kaleidoscopic view.

Now that we have theorised and considered the scope of our problem, we will briefly consider one system-thinking approach that of Kania et al. (2018), six conditions of systems change. At the base level of the system, Kania et al. (2018) position the transformative change: implicit mental models. The mental models are where we find common sense understandings, the taken-for-granted knowledge, and traditionally held beliefs and values that influence how we act, think, and respond to the problem (Carne et al., 2019) of technology-mediated intimate abuse and arguments located in this chapter. The next layer is semi-explicit, where we find power dynamics and relationship constructions. Power dynamics are fundamental in any system as this is the location of any decision-making authority in both formal and non-formal individuals and organisations and where change can occur (Carne et al., 2019). This is where it becomes instrumental in including stakeholders and policymakers in research due to the positions and power, they hold to effect change. Relationships and connections: This aspect of the system is where partnerships and the qualities of relationships between the network are imperative to its success, drawing on the differing viewpoints and histories to provide the broadest scope. At the highest level, we have explicit structural change—policies, practices, and resource flows. These three combined have the most influence over the system and where broader societal change can occur. Resource flows relate to money, people, knowledge, and broader assets, which can be allocated and distributed to work on the problem. Practices encompass entities (procedures, guidelines, shared ideas/habits), institutions, and networks that inform and/or influence the problem (Carne et al., 2019). Policies: The rules, regulations, policies, and priorities of institutions and governments that guide the work and influence others' actions (Carne et al., 2019). Within these six conditions for system change, researchers can begin considering adopting tactics and utilising approaches to unpacking what technologically mediated intimate partner abuse is, in line with a system-thinking approach

to elicit a positive change over time. As we can see from the six conditions of system change, the argument located within this section of the
chapter on language and definition is the first step to eliciting effective
change.

Conclusion

In summary, this chapter has aimed to introduce the reader to theoretical
pluralism when considering researching technologically mediated intimate partner abuse with systems thinking as the main driver. Systems
thinking as a mechanism of social change has been illustrated throughout
this chapter as a driving force for stakeholders, policymakers, researchers,
and others to bring to fruition the most challenging and complex
issues currently facing society today within a framework utilising a
common focus and goal. In particular, I have argued for the meanings
of technology and technological objects to include both the literal and
metaphorical in the analysis to ensure the whole meaning of these objects
can reflect the lived realities of the users from both the perspective of a
perpetrator and a victim/survivor. Overall, it is possible to conclude that
adopting a system approach to researching technology to mediate intimate partner abuse can allow for transformation change in the long run
and a deeper understanding of the issue at hand presented from several
vantage points.

Key Recommendations

1. Adoption of theoretical pluralism when researching and considering
   technology-mediated intimate partner abuse to consider the possibilities between the self, behaviours, motivations, and technologies.
2. Clarifying language and definition, within and between stakeholders,
   policymakers, legislation, and researchers more succulently, to help
   develop and clarify an understanding of 'tech abuse' beyond domestic
   abuse.

3. For systems thinking to be considered in the application and design of digital objects, to move beyond the literal to the metaphorical for more explicit consideration of how technologies and/or digital objects can be used in intimate abuse, with the recognition of the current inequalities between technologies of tools of abuse and technologies as tools of support (Kellam, 2020).

4. Reflection of service delivery modules or services that have not been evaluated in the last 3–5 years, to be re-evaluated using system thinking to help agencies and services understand which interventions are working well and for whom, as well as which are not and why.

References

Bachman, R. (2000). A comparison of annual incident rates and contextual characteristics of intimate-partner violence against women from the national crime victimisation survey and the national violence against women survey. *Violence Against, 6*(1), 839–867.

Barthes, R. (1957). *Mythologies*. Hill & Wang Publishing.

Bender, A. (2017). Ethics, methods, and measures in intimate partner violence research: The current state of the field. *Violence Against Women, 23*(11), 1382–1413.

Berg, A. J. (1999). A gendered socio-technical construction: The smart house. In D. Mackenzie & J. Wajcman (Eds.), *The social shaping of technologies* (2nd ed.). Open University Press.

Bond, E. (2014). *Childhood, mobile technologies and everyday experiences changing technologies = Changing childhoods?* Palgrave Macmillan.

Burgess-Proctor, A. (2015). Methodological and ethical issues in feminist research with abused women: Reflections on participants' vulnerability and empowerment. *Women's Studies International Forum, 48*(1), 124–134.

Callen, M., & Latour, B. (1981). Unscrewing the Big Leviathan: How actors macro-structure reality and how sociologists help them do so. In K. Knorr-Cetina & A. V. Cicourel (Eds.), *Advances in social theory and methodology toward an integration of micro and macro sociologies*. Routledge and Kegan Paul.

Carne, S., Rees, D., Paton, N., & Fanslow, J. (2019). *Using systems thinking to address intimate partner violence and child abuse in New Zealand*. https://nzfvc.org.nz/sites/nzfvc.org.nz/files/NZFVC-issues-paper-13-systems-thinking.pdf. Accessed 29 August 2023.

Castells, M. (1996). *The rise of network society, the information age: Economy, society and culture* (Vol. I). Blackwell.

Castells, M. (1997). *The power of identity, the information age: Economy, society and culture* (Vol. II). Blackwell.

Castells, M. (2000). *The rise of network society* (2nd ed.). Blackwell.

Castells, M. (2004). The network society: A cross-cultural perspective. Edward Elgar Publishing Ltd

Christie, L., & Wright, S. (2020). *Technology and abuse*. https://post.parliament.uk/technology-and-domestic-abuse/. Accessed 2 September 2023.

Domestic Abuse Act, 2021 (c. 17).

Foucault, M. (1975). *Discipline and punish: The birth of the prison* (A. Sheridan, Trans.) Allen Lane, Penguin.

Fraga, S. (2016). Methodological and ethical challenges in violence research. *Porto Biomedical Journal, 1*(2), 77–80.

George, A., & Harris, B. (2014). *Landscapes of violence: Women surviving family violence in regional and rural Victoria*. https://www.deakin.edu.au/__data/assets/pdf_file/0003/287040/Landscapes-of-Violence-online-pdf-version.pdf. Accessed 9 March 2020.

Gomm, R. (2008). *Social research methodology.* Palgrave Macmillan.

Hang, T., Chung, D., & Peters, M. (2009). *The use of information and communication technologies to coerce and control in domestic violence and following separation*. https://pdfs.semanticscholar.org/c4ce/8b1b3bd958da4320ee65ec5bc4f271862a86.pdf. Accessed 9 March 2020.

Harris, B. (2018). Spacelessness, spatiality and intimate partner violence technology—Facilitated abuse, stalking and justice administration. In K. Fitz-Gibbon, S. Walklate, J. McCulloch, & J. M. Maher (Eds.), *Securing women's lives in a global world* (pp. 52–70). Routledge.

Hess, A. (2015). The selfie assemblage. *International Journal of Communication, 9*(1), 1629–1646.

Hutchby, I., & Moran-Ellis, J. (2001). Introduction: Relating children technology and culture. In I. Hutchby & J. Moran-Ellis (Eds.), *Children, technology and culture: The impacts of technologies in children's everyday lives.* Routledge Falmer.

Inglis, D., & Thorpe, C. (2019). *An invitation to social theory* (2nd ed.). Polity Press.

Kania, J., Kramer, M., & Senge, P. (2018). *The water of system change*. http://efc.issuelab.org/resources/30855/30855.pdf. Accessed 4 September 2023.

Kaplan, G., Diez Roux, A., Simon, C., & Galea, S. (2017). *Growing inequality bridging complex systems, population health and health disparities*. Westphalia Press.

Kellam, A. (2020). Domestic abuse during the UK's COVID-19 Lockdown: From normal to new normal and what survivors' experiences might teach us. *Amicus Curiae, 1*(3), 361–378.

Kline, R., & Pinch, T. (1999). The social construction of technology. In D. MacKenzie & J. Wajcman (Eds.), *The social shaping of technology* (2nd ed.). Open University Press.

Latour, B. (1996). On actor-network theory. A few clarifications plus more than a few complications. *Soziale Welt, 47*, 369–381.

Latour, B. (1999). On recalling ANT. In J. Law & J. Hassard (Eds.), *Actor network theory and after* (pp. 15–25). Blackwell.

Latour, B. (2000). 'When thing strike back: A possible contribution of "science studies" to the social sciences. *British Journal of Sociology, 51*(1), 107–123.

Law, J. (1997). *Traduction/trahison: Notes on ACT*. Centre for Science Studies, Lancaster University. http://www.comp.lancs.ac.uk/sociology/papers/Law-Traduction-Trahison.pdf

Law, J. (2003). Notes on the theory of the actor network: Ordering, strategy and heterogeneity. *Systems Practice, 5*(4), 379–393.

Ling, R. (2012). *Taken for grantedness: The embedding of mobile communication into society*. MIT Press.

Mackenzie, D., & Wajcman, J. (Eds.). (1999). *The Social Shaping of Technology* (2nd ed.). Open University Press.

Matthewman, S. (2011). *Technology and social theory*. Palgrave MacMillan.

Meadows, D. (2008). *Thinking in systems: A primer*. Chelsea Green Publishing.

Mirrlees-Black, C. (1999). *Domestic violence: Findings from a new British crime survey self-completion questionnaire*. Home Office Research Study No.1991, Research, Development and Statistics Directorate. Home Office.

Mirrlees-Black, C. (1995). *Estimating the extent of domestic violence: Findings from the 1992 British crime survey*. Home Office Research Bulletin 37.

Myerson, G. (2001). *Heidegger, Habermas and the mobile phone*. Icon Books.

Rittel, H. W., & Webber, M. M. (1973). Dilemmas in a general theory of planning. *Policy Sciences, 4*(2), 155–169.

Schwarz, O. (2021). *Sociological theory for digital society*. Polity Press.

Shapiro, S. (1998). Places and spaces: The historical interaction of technology, home and privacy. *The Information and Society, 14*(4), 275–284.

Stroh, D. P. (2015). *Systems thinking for social change: A practical guide to solving complex problems, avoiding unintended consequences, and achieving lasting results.* Chelsea Green Publishing.

In Search of Hopes for Change: What Can Systems Thinking Offer Racial Justice-Oriented Networks Aimed at Tackling Systemic Invisibility of Black, Brown, and Other Racially Minoritised Voices in the VAWG/DASV Sphere

Meena Kumari and Olumide Adisa

Introduction

The murder of George Floyd in the United States in 2020 sparked protests across the globe calling for racial justice. Following this Breonna Taylor, a 26-year-old Black American woman, was fatally shot in her Louisville, Kentucky apartment on March 13, 2020, when at least seven police officers forced entry into the apartment as part of an investigation into drug dealing operations and was unjustly killed by the police in her home. These tragic events would lead to declarations and discussions on systemic racism in the US, and globally.

M. Kumari (✉) · O. Adisa
H.O.P.E Training and Consultancy, Leicester, UK
e-mail: admin@hopetraining.co.uk

O. Adisa
e-mail: o.adisa@uos.ac.uk

O. Adisa
Institute of Social Justice and Crime, University of Suffolk, Ipswich, UK

Here in the UK, it also brought into sharp focus, the issue of systemic institutional racism, which is embedded structurally in all our institutions. Concerning violence against Black women, this issue was amplified by the tragic murders of Bibaa Henry (aged 46) and Nicole Smallman (aged 27), two sisters who were stabbed to death by Danyal Hussein in Fryent Country Park, Kingsbury, north-west London, England, on 6 June 2020 and the police failings and the lack of media attention given to the killing of Black women.

In 2023, the Baroness Louise Casey's final report into the Metropolitan Police found severe institutional failings across the organisation that will require radical reform to resolve. The Crossbench Peer was commissioned to review the culture and standards of London's police service in the wake of the rape, abduction, and murder of Sarah Everard by a serving Metropolitan police officer, and a series of other scandals that have shattered public confidence and trust in the police force. Following a year-long investigation, in her final and full report, Baroness Casey laid bare deep and wide shortcomings across the force including compelling evidence that there is institutional racism, sexism and homophobia, inside the organisation in terms of how officers and staff are treated, and outside the organisation in terms of how communities are policed (Casey, 2023).

In this chapter, we define racial justice as a vision for attaining racial equity through transforming systems. Racial equity relates to the intentional and sustained practice of changing discriminatory policies, structures, and systems affecting racially minoritised communities.

Racial Justice Allyship in VAWG Sphere in the Wake of Black Lives Matter Protests

All these tragic events earlier mentioned were happening during the Covid-19 pandemic crisis, which resulted in a combination of adopting, then easing, lockdown measures that restricted movement, and increased reports of 'ethnic minorities' elevated risk of contagion and death. The UK was amidst a public health and social crisis, strained further by familial and economic tensions. Less discussed were the psychological trauma of these events on already vulnerable people, specifically racialised communities who are suffering domestic abuse, and the implications for their safety (Khan et al., 2020)— and the H.O.P.E[1] national calls provided a *hopeful* forum to have those conversations about the impact of racial prejudice, the highly publicised race-related violence and what it means for Black and minoritised women.

No one institution in the UK is immune to systemic racism. These crisis events also shifted the focus inwards to examine and tackle anti-racism issues in the VAWG/DASV sphere.

In the next section, we discuss the key ideas guiding our analysis in this chapter.

Theorising *Hopes for Change*

Hope theory was developed by psychologist Charles Snyder in the 1990s. Hope results from individuals perceived capability to develop goal thoughts and pathways for achieving them (Snyder, 1994, 2000).

Darren Webb identifies a distinction between two meta-modes of hoping, relating to: 'goal-oriented hope', and 'open-ended hope' (Webb, 2007, p. 68). In this chapter, our idea of *hopes for change* relates to both, in an ongoing reflexive and collaborative process of 'documenting hopeful possibilities' (Back, 2021, p. 1).

Speaking of change in hopeful terms also aligns with a feminist characterisation of hope (Coleman & Ferreday, 2010). History has shown that the dismantling of oppressive systems is possible through sustained collective efforts of those that society places on the margins or minoritises across time and space as well as through sustained allyship.

Raynor opines that 'hope is not a singular and fixed concept' (Raynor, 2021, p. 553). As such, we opine that hope can be viewed as a part of the energy of a system, which (re)shapes system behaviour and relational

---

[1] This chapter draws inspiration from the acronym H.O.P.E in reflecting on the notion of hopes for changes as a theoretical concept. The organisation H.O.P.E stands for Helping Other People Every day and is a national Training and consultancy provider, founded by Meena Kumari, and is based in the Midlands specialising in VAWG anti-racism training as well as safeguarding training.

power dynamics towards change, for example, through equitable power and resource flows. Black feminist bell hooks opine that hope energises during struggles of freedom. In her words,

> Hopefulness empowers us to continue our work for justice even as the forces of injustice may gain power for a time. To live by hope is to believe that it is worth taking the next step. (hooks, 2003, pp. xiv–xv)

Here in this chapter, we position our hopes for changes as a type of work, and labour that deserves surfacing, taking inspiration from what Les Back calls *Hope's Work*. He notes:

> Hope, then is an empirical question, and a matter of documenting hopeful possibilities that often otherwise remain unremarked upon. (Back, 2021, p. 1)

The labour that goes into changing systems deserves to be remarked upon, and as result, our hopeful encounters with all those that continuously participated in the H.O.P.E national calls and supported this work, have been a been a central point of inspiration for this chapter. We all owe a debt of gratitude to many women (and men) who undertake work within racialised communities that often go unremarked upon by the system.

In the next sections, we briefly discuss the sector's response and use a systems thinking concept (specifically systems leadership), to surface hopeful possibilities for racial-justice-oriented practice in the VAWG/DASV sphere.

Black Lives Matter, the Anti-Racism Charter, Systems Leadership, in the VAWG/DASV Sphere

The racial justice system-oriented response that was undertaken within the VAWG/DASV sector during the two-year period (2020–2022) can be described as something akin to episodic allyship, which we have coined due to its mirroring of episodic system change efforts. As described by Foster-Fishman and Behrens (2007), episodic change efforts show huge promise but become truncated or stunted due to lack of funding, energy, and capacity issues, and as such are not able to be sustained. We posit that episodic allyship is different from performative allyship[2] although both are just as problematic in stalling change efforts. In the next subsumed paragraphs, we further make this point, using our observations of the Black Lives Matter (BLM) statements made particularly by the large white-led VAWG organisations (often called 'second-tier organisations'), as an example.

These organisations tend to hold a lot of power and resources, at least in comparison to community-based 'by and for' specialist organisations who remain woefully underfunded based on previous research on the VAWG/DASV funding ecosystem (Adisa et al., 2020; Imkaan, 2018). These power and resource flows are important in understanding 'what/who' gets visibility, and 'what/who' is relatively invisibilised.

During the widely publicised racial justice protests, many large organisations in the UK would also make their own declarations on 'Black Lives Matter' and issue compelling statements on social media acknowledging these systemic inequities and expressing solidarity. However, this immediate public show of solidarity was notably absent in the VAWG/DASV sector in the UK. Depending on who you ask, it is a matter of debate as to whether this urgency-defying approach was the right one.[3]

In Sept/Oct 2021, the VAWG Anti-Racism Charter ('the Charter') was launched and spearheaded by two second-tier organisations— Imkaan and End Violence Against Women (EVAW). Seven relatively

---

[2] Performative allyship refers to when 'someone from a non-margainalised group professing support and solidarity with a marginalised group' (Kalina, 2020, p. 478) which is motivated by reward (profits, and virtue signalling as examples).

[3] For instance, it could be argued that a thoughtful approach required some time to secure commitments from larger, white-led organisations, which likely enabled campaign organisers to avoid the performative allyship issue which emerged with the use/misuse of the 'Black squares' (a symbol showing support for Black lives during global protests) by white influencers on social media (see Wellman, 2022).

influential VAWG charities (all led by women CEOs) published a statement in support of the Charter in October 2021.[4] This system-oriented response is a noteworthy breakthrough and potentially offers many hopes for changes.

Nonetheless, we viewed the Charter with some degree of scepticism as we were not able to ascertain whether there is a clear plan for how those that sign up to the Charter will fund the work they have committed to undertake. There is a present risk of this initiative being a persistent case of episodic allyship, and an unintended consequence of systems change.

As earlier mentioned, we choose to believe that these allyship statements of support for the Charter are not performative and that (through a 'hopes for changes' lens) the white-led organisations[5] in the group genuinely care about racial justice and race equity issues and want to see transformational change. Based on our personal experiences thus far we can for sure say this about two out of the seven organisations, who signed the statement below.[6]

In their words,

We are speaking up as the CEOs of second tier membership organisations of the women's sector and particularly the ending male violence against women and girls' sector.

We support the recently launched VAWG Anti-Racism Charter.

Firstly, we acknowledge the critical point in time at which we write, the worldwide public visibility of the murder of George Floyd, the campaigning of Black Lives Matter and the spotlight shone on racial violence and structural inequality.

---

[4] It is possible that more organisations quietly signed up, so we ask the reader to exercise caution in interpreting this as the full sample.

[5] White-led organisations refer to those led by a white CEO. At the time of writing, Safelives was led by a mixed-heritage CEO, based on published diversity data.

[6] Through our collaborative work, we have had direct experience of two of the seven organisations during this time. We have both collaborated with Respect and Safelives on different projects (e.g., diversifying the sector and anti-racism training, MARACs, Call to action to name a few), and so we have had a closer encounter through engagement with some Staff and management, and our own experience of engaging with these two organisations' CEOs. This is not to say that we 'fully know' these organisations or that their Black and other minoritised Staff have these same positive experiences.

*We also acknowledge the 40th anniversary of the New Cross Massacre of black children and young people without consequence for the perpetrators and the trauma caused by these and continuing acts along the continuum of daily racism. As we understand the continuum of sexist violence, so we understand the continuum of racist violence. Both are woven deeply.—**Excerpt from the statement signed by 7 large women-sector/VAWG organisations**[7]* (Rape Crisis England & Wales, 2021)

For this chapter, we collated and examined the types of commitments made by these eight white-led organisations between 2021 and 2022 on their external websites, and whether this led to a clear plan or action which was then publicly published for accountability. Since signing the Charter, the degree to which all these organisations have acted has varied, which have implications for accountability and transparency, and more importantly for sustained allyship and systems leadership on racial justice matters in white-led organisations in VAWG/DASV. While space does not permit a full analysis here, in the next section, we discuss a case study to highlight the ways that systems leadership can manifest.

Case Study: Systems Leadership on Racial Justice in VAWG/DASV Charities

Systems leadership relates to the skills, capacities, and values for leading systems change within institutions and communities (Hopkins & Higham, 2007; Government Office for Science, 2023). Specifically in the VAWG/DASV sphere, systems leadership has previously been conceptualised as a necessary condition for systems change (Adisa et al., 2023a).

---

[7] Full list of organisations that signed the statement: Imkaan, Rape Crisis England & Wales, Women's Resource Centre, Welsh Women's Aid, Women's Aid Federation of England, End Violence Against Women Coalition, and Respect.

In 2020, Safelives[8] provided support/funding for the national H.O.P.E calls. Similarly, the DRIVE partnership[9] supported scoping work to capture insights and knowledge on working with those who use harmful behaviours in racialised communities. Three years on from the initial support this work, these organisations have been sustained allies to our academic-practitioner collaboration.

It is interesting to note that Safelives did not wait a year (or for the launch of the Charter) to act but rather recognised the importance of galvanising hopes for changes in that pivotal moment to drive systems change within their own organisation, specifically with respect to anti-Black racism. The organisation took two visible actions and then publicly published this for accountability. The first was the very detailed Equity, Equality, Diversity, and Inclusion (EEDI) plan and the second was their public response[10] to the now discredited government-backed race report, Commission on Race and Ethnic Disparities[11] ('Safelives' detailed response to the Race Report', u.d.).

> *Too few individuals and organisations have been carrying the burden of tackling racism and bringing attention to issues of race on their own for too long. Since this report was released, we've heard frustration, anger and sadness from those who have been doing this work relentlessly for many years. We are adding our voice in solidarity.* (Excerpt from 'Safelives' detailed response to the Race Report,' u.d.[12])

---

[8] Led by its CEO, Suzanne Jacob (at the time of writing, this post is in recruitment for a new CEO).

[9] Drive partnership is a White-led organisation, and comprises of Respect, Safelives, and Social Finance.

[10] Safelives signed an open letter of charity leaders (with over 2000 signatories) from across different sectors, spearheaded by Runnymede Trust challenging the report findings and which led to the social media #RejecttheReport campaign. Due to the legal sensitivities around the open letter, we were not able to access a copy at the time of writing this paper to examine how many other VAWG organisations signed the letter.

[11] In response to the Black Lives Matter protests, the then Prime Minister Boris Johnson commissioned the 'Commission on Race and Ethnic Disparities' report. With the wide public backlash on the report's findings, the government has since tried to distance itself from the report.

[12] https://safelives.org.uk/detailed_response_race_report.

Safelives was the only VAWG organisation that made a public response as a signatory to the open letter and, in fact, used the opportunity to link this stance to their EEDI plan and their ongoing commitment to racial justice.

To date, they are the only second-tier VAWG organisation to have used their influence to help drive financial support for the H.O.P.E national calls, which have now morphed into cross-cultural webinars (which ended in 2023). Systems leadership requires an intentional and sustained effort to build racial equity into the system.

Yet, as demonstrated in the published report in August 2023,[13] Safelives had independently commissioned Kaveed Ali, Director of EEDI at UK Community Foundations, to review Safelives' progress towards becoming an anti-racist organisation and found significant shortcomings. Ali's key findings were that:

> The organisation is divided in its ambition and sense of purpose around anti-racism. SafeLives lacks a shared understanding of what anti-racism means strategically and operationally. The organisation lacks some of the core capabilities to deliver this work. There are high levels of fear around anti-racism and what it might mean. Organisational culture is the key obstacle to delivering change. (Safelives, 2023)

Ali's findings suggest that even where there is committed systems leadership on anti-racist practice, bringing about systems change takes time, and that without a sense of interconnectedness and a shared purpose, a system misalignment issue ensues which inhibits the gains which good systems leadership can bring.

---

[13] https://safelives.org.uk/EEDI/2021-22.

Promoting System Visibility for Black, Brown, and Other Racially Minoritised Voices

In April 2020, the national H.O.P.E Zoom Calls/Webinars were set up looking at domestic abuse within Black and minoritised communities during Covid-19. H.O.P.E network now has over 250 members.

The national H.O.P.E Calls centred the voices of Black and minoritised professionals working in the VAWG/DASV sector. While the aim of these online network meetups and the shift to online space was precipitated by Covid-19, the calls for racial justice sparked by the tragic murder of George Floyd even further catapulted this work onto the mainstream, and this transformative power of a shared vision and purpose is interesting and deserves reflection.

In the next section, we discuss this intentional and hopeful approach which we have termed during our reflections as a 'dialogical-intersectional feminist gathering (DIFG)', due to our acceptance of the gendered nature of domestic abuse, intersectionality, and the primacy of equitable dialogue within the calls and webinars. In this chapter, we have used this concept to deepen our reflections.

This DIFG helped professionals working in the domestic abuse and sexual violence (DASV) sector to encounter narratives on racial justice-oriented practice during and beyond the crisis. The DIFG became a fertile ground for activating culturally responsive awareness within the system, involving over eighty speakers in 2020, and generated an evidence base the 'discussions, 'reflections', and 'actions' that emerged (Adisa & Khan, 2021).

The DIFG also provided a site for foregrounding the ethics of responsibility towards the Self-*Other*—providing an opportunity for the empowered *Self-Other* to be positioned as the receiver, as against the norm of viewing Other as receiver and less powerful.[14] Through this

---

[14] This approach towards an ethics of responsibility to the Other has been inspired by Bakhtin's concept of otherness and Levinas' 'infinite' other. Bakhtin, M. M. (1986). *Methodology for the human sciences. Speech genres and other late essays* (Emerson, C., & Holquist, M., Eds., V. W. McGee, Trans., pp. 159–172). University of Texas Press; and Levinas, E. (1978). *Existence and existents* (A. Lingis, Trans.). Nijhoff, respectively. The idea of a Self-Other configuration as against the conventional dichotomy of Self/Other draws on Henry-Waring, M. S.

collaborative DIFG, we were able to pay more attention to hopeful possibilities about change, in challenging times—as voiced by the Black and Brown women who used the calls to amplify their voices. In these (Kumari's) words:

A place of **hopes**, where seldom heard Black and Brown voices were neither forced to whisper or were hushed by more prominent voices already seated at the decision-making table. Hidden and grassroots voices were empowered, because they were heard and understood without fear of judgment or reprisal.

For the rest of the chapter, where we use 'DIFG', we mean the H.O.P.E Calls, and vice versa.

Hopeful Possibilities: A Re-emergence of Intersectional Equity Building in the VAWG/ DASV Sphere

The intersecting issues of anti-racism, inequalities, and VAWG/DASV concerns gained remarkable visibility in 2020, and rightly so. In her 2016 paper, Marai Larasi traces the early network-building efforts of 'by and for' specialist services in the 1970s and 1980s (Larasi, 2016, p. 269), and she argues that Black and minoritised women had to navigate two distinct systems to bring to the centre (as against being on the margins) the specialist knowledge to tackle pressing issues of the multiple forms of oppression (intersectionality), and anti-racism activism on the other. Yet as she points out, it is not as simple as it sounds, in that women from racialised communities were not a homogeneous group but held divergent political positions which often resulted in tensions and

---

(2017). *Moving beyond otherness: (Re)vealing, (re)centring and (re)inscribing the polyvocal subjectivities of African Caribbean women across the United Kingdom* (Thesis). Monash University. https://doi.org/10.4225/03/589ab569c6a39. **A more thorough discussion can be found in Adisa, O. 'Centring Otherness with migrant women affected by domestic abuse' in Otherness in Communication Research: Perspectives in Media, Interpersonal, and Intercultural Communication (forthcoming).**

disagreements for Black and minoritised feminists in the wider feminist movement.

Larasi further opines that 'these contentions were not always addressed or resolved leading to fractures within as well as disconnections between organisations' (p. 272). More importantly, she highlights some of the tough decisions that 'by and for' organisations took to ensure their survival over the years, and which continue to plague many 'by and for' organisations today. For example, the erosion and loss of connection to social justice grassroots (organising roots) as well as what powerful actors (like large funders) ascribe 'value' to (ibid.).

Both intersectionality and ethnicity specificity featured in many of the DIFG conversations. Intersectionality is an analytical framework developed by the Black feminist legal theorist Kimberlé Crenshaw as a corrective to the limitations of then-dominant single-axis models of gender and race discrimination. Crenshaw observed that these models obscured the complexities of racialised gender discrimination (and gendered racial discrimination) experienced by Black women (Crenshaw, 1989). This thinking on interlocking systems of oppression experienced by Black women is thought to have originated from the Combahee River Collective in the 1970s. In practice, there is more understanding of intersectionality in the shaping of service delivery perspective in the VAWG/DASV sphere, thanks to Imkaan's intersectional feminist writings (Larasi, 2016), as well as the campaigning and advocacy efforts of many Black, Brown, and other minoritised women like Sistah Space, Amour Destiné, PHOEBE, Halo Project, Sikh Women's Aid, Kijiji, Hersana, and more. And if you are reading this chapter, we want to say that: We see you, and that we appreciate you.

Ethnicity specificity relates to the greater awareness of the ethnic lumping labelling issue (use of labels like 'BAME', 'BME') which collapses the unique experiences of diverse racial groups (which differ due to their ethnic identities, and culture) into one homogenous category, and the barriers to reporting and help-seeking for Black women of African and Caribbean heritage, in particular. Additionally, a summary of our research findings has shown that this labelling practice particularly invisibilises Black women[15] in the multiple systems relating to VAWG/DASV (Adisa & Khan, 2021). The next section discusses the range of topics that featured in the DIFG.

The HOPE Calls as a Systems Change Response to Promoting Cross-cultural Understanding

The range of topics discussed at the DIFG was wide-ranging. Issues such as the Domestic Abuse Bill, depleted funding of support services, no recourse to public funds for migrant women, and racial discrimination in the domestic abuse sector as well as within services were all covered. Victim experiences, including rape, sexual abuse and exploitation, hidden harms in faith-based communities, spiritual abuse, witchcraft, coercive control, male victims, and housing issues, were also examined in the discussions.

Building on the success of the online DIFG gatherings, virtual cross-cultural training (CCT) webinars were developed. H.O.P.E recognised that cultural competence should be a core requirement across the VAWG/DASV sector, helping organisations better understand and respond to the needs of Black, Asian, and other minoritised victims of domestic abuse, so with funding by a large funder Lloyds TSB Foundation (supported by Safelives), H.O.P.E developed 12 webinars all speakers from Black, Asian, or minoritised backgrounds running from March 2021 to November 2021. The average attendance was 110.

In one independent evaluation undertaken by researchers at the University of Suffolk, the researchers conducted pre- and post-training online survey data collected from participants—demographic details, profession, expectations for the training, confidence, and knowledge (five-point Likert scale) and had open-ended responses regarding participants' views of the cross-cultural training (CCT) session. They also

---

[15] By this, we mean Black women racialised as Black due to their physical characteristics and who face colourism and bias, due to their dark skin colour/complexion.

conducted virtual interviews with 10 CCT trainers—recorded and transcribed using speech to-text software. One key finding was that the CCT had a predominantly White audience (approx. 78%), and only 36% had previously received training on cultural competency which only 19% had received guidance and help from their employer in relation to working with racially minoritised clients and most participants were in frontline roles or work within statutory, health, or educational services (Adisa et al., 2022).[16]

Another key theme from the CCT project was that there is a clear need for CCT, and that lack of attention to this need has negatively impacted responses to culturally and racially minoritised survivors. This may not be a surprise to some, particularly those in organisations previously mentioned who have devoted great effort in calling out racism in the VAWG/DASV spaces that they occupy.

The linking of systems thinking concepts to this racial justice work to drive systemic change in equity terms only came about through exploring the hopeful possibilities of systems thinking in the DASV sphere through this chapter. Our ongoing academic-practitioner collaboration during the pandemic catalysed systems change conversations in developing culturally responsive approaches, with the specific communities affected. This focus on specificity of minoritised ethnic identities (in the global majority) has been long overdue.

There is no doubt that our own similar yet also different experiences of racism in the VAWG/DASV sector, academia, and housing (and in navigating everyday life) have shaped how we approach our scholarship, activism, and practice. While we both share a deep commitment to social justice, and this is evident from our work over the last two decades, the dual crisis of the Covid-19 and the murder of George Floyd, and the policing failures in the murder of Bibba Henry and Nicole Smallman will come to further infuse a radical hope perspective to our work. Our jointly shared personal motto became one of *multiplied hopes* that the time to do something radical and system shifting is not in the future but, now.

---

[16] The second CCT evaluation (Allen et al., 2023) was completed in 2023 and corroborated the earlier findings in the 2022 report.

Collective hopeful encounters became a necessity for sustaining racial justice-oriented systems change, especially considering the costs of racial trauma including weathering.[17] We recognise that there is a personal and professional cost involved in developing networks and initiatives that aim to bring about racial-justice-oriented systems change when we encounter and must navigate institutionally racist structures ourselves. As expressed authentically in the words below:

> I'm getting tired of the DASV sector becoming defensive when they hear the word racism or anti-racism about who they are and the belief that we all have about ourselves that we are good people, we need to recognise this is not about morals, or about who is good or bad- this is about the DASV sector recognising and acknowledging that we have and are upholding a whole system that disadvantages certain voices and to really do the work, to examine what part does your organisation play in reproducing this disadvantage, intentionally or unintentionally? Accountability structures in the VAWG/DASV sphere are desperately needed.—Kumari's verbatim reflections (in dialogue with Adisa, January 2023)

In Search of Hopes for (Systems) Change: Concluding Remarks

More than two years on, the dual crisis has become a multiple crisis (Covid-19, systemic racism, and cost of living), and as the H.O.P.E national calls come to an end in 2023, we find ourselves asking whether the gains achieved in this DIFG are at risk of being rolled back in a post-Covid recovery phase, particularly in relation to the marginalisation and blotting out of voices of Black, Asian, and other minoritised victims/survivors and practitioners in the VAWG/DASV sector.

Yet we hold things in *hope*, that the ethos of the H.O.P.E national calls in relation to holding and reclaiming space are retained and that

---

[17] Weathering is a term coined by Arline T. Geronimus to describe the toll on physical body resulting from persistent systemic injustices (Geronimus, 2023).

the ethics of responsibility which shaped its existence, long continues in some shape and form.

With the increasing return of face-to-face events, there are ongoing conversations about the need for virtual safe spaces like the H.O.P.E national calls, and what the loss of virtual safe spaces which emerged during the height of the crisis, and what this means for dimensions of access such as accessibility and affordability[18] which affect different people (e.g., disabled people, those who are immunocompromised or care for those who are, and those who are low-waged among others). On the other hand, the huge benefits of holding virtual spaces can often be negated by the digital access implications for those who dwell in areas with low internet connectivity and/or smartphones, who may be deprived access to informal and formal virtual spaces[19] and for survivors who may be in refuges or other similar arrangements. We highlight these considerations for those that may wish to set up a similar DIFG in the future.

This chapter has argued that tackling systems invisibility[20] of racialised communities in systems change calls for a reimagining of systems change in equity terms—an equitable *system* is one that values Black, Brown, and racially minoritised voices in systems change efforts within the VAWG/DASV sphere. We questioned the emergence of episodic allyship and further argued for sustained allyship as a fundamental aspect to systems leadership, and as an important ingredient for achieving racial equity collectively.

We do not purport to have all the answers. However, we have shown in this paper that much can be better understood through fusing systems thinking, a theorised hope (*hopes for changes*), sustained allyship, racial

---

[18] See Penchansky and Thomas (1981) for the concepts of access mentioned here.

[19] For example, these issues relating to digital access are already having ramifications in the socio-legal sphere in relation to remote justice (Adisa et al., 2023a, b).

[20] System invisibility, as a term, transcends reductive terms such as representation with respect to numbers. By system visibility, we mean letting people speak with their own mouths and valuing their labour and knowledges (in case we are not clear, let Black women speak for themselves; and let Brown women speak for themselves). We mean using one's privilege to position many critical marginalised voices in sites of power and influence; and to practically support their work with funding and resources to engender participation in systems change conversations.

justice, and systems leadership, in any blueprint for long-term systems change.

The pace of change is slowing, and this chapter is a clarion call to (re)illuminate the focus on racial equity and justice as an ever-present urgency which we must not lose sight of. Our vision relies on a hope-fuelled systems-oriented perspective that is underpinned by a purposeful network of change makers and sustained allies. We invite you the reader to join us.

With a hope-oriented ethical grounding, the systemic nature of racism (which relates to multiple complex systems) calls for new conceptual tools that centre the notion of critiquing, disrupting, and overhauling the system as well as uncovering attitudes and behaviours that are incompatible with truly embedding equity in the system.

It is not all doom and gloom, and our notion of '*hopes for changes*' (represented here in this text), requires a sustained movement of systems leaders to transform the system for the better. This requires a concerted effort to make the VAWG/DASV sector more inclusive and equitable. We are hopeful for a system transformation that is committed to an equitable distribution of power and resources, coupled with a practice of continued self-reflection on overt and covert privileges held by white-led organisations, to tackle relative system invisibility of Black, Brown, and other racially minoritised voices.

We are beginning to see sustained allyship on this issue in innovative ways—for example, through the national systems change work on domestic abuse perpetration, that the Drive partnership[21] is undertaking, and as corroborated through an independent systems change evaluation by the University of Suffolk, which has recently been completed.[22]

We hope to continue to encourage visible accountability and transparent mechanisms of change to better understand the impacts of system-wide changes to tackling systemic racism and injustices, and to centre the voices and needs of those at the margins in VAWG/DASV spaces.

---

[21] The partnership comprises of three organisations Safelives, Respect, and Social Finance.
[22] Adisa et al. (2023a, b).

In future writings, we hope to further capture other intentional systemic change efforts in the DASV sphere as examples, as there are likely to be other fascinating examples which space precludes doing this justice here. Additionally, we have been thinking more about how to systematise a theorised 'hopes for changes' to act *as* reinforcing and balancing feedback loops[23] in transforming the system through safe(r) spaces, but this will need further exposition beyond the scope of this chapter. Additionally, in relation to funding systems leadership, how might large funders help build equity by funding long-term projects on anti-racism and VAWG/DASV concerns? This would require a commitment to support specialist 'by and for' grassroots who wish to reconnect with their activist and campaigning roots without the fear of being seen as too radical, or inefficient due to their small size. The point we wish to make here is that there is ample opportunity to further theorise, research, and document multiplied and dynamic hopes for changes through systems change endeavours in VAWG/DASV sphere. We cannot afford to run out of energy.

We end this chapter, in the way that we began, (and unsurprisingly) with *hope*. As the earlier quote from Safelives highlighted, the struggle for racial justice and the recognition of systemic racism did not begin in 2020 but has spanned decades, and we pay tribute to the many intersectional feminists that have historically undertaken this emotional and energy-sapping labour, sometimes without a remarkable breakthrough, funnelling through what Patricia Hill Collins calls a *politics of empowerment* (Collins, 2022). Here in this chapter, we have shown that much can be accomplished through synthesising systems thinking, *hopes for change* (foregrounded by an ethics of responsibility to the Self-Other), as well as recognising that we operate in a system that is made up of a constellation of interconnections and relationships. We boldly opine that a responsive systems thinking-oriented approach has much to offer building equity and shifting power dynamics, as highlighted through the

---

[23] Reinforcing and balancing feedback typically describe how systems evolve over time and are represented by circular structures, which represent the complex dynamics of change (for a thorough discussion, see Stroh [2015]).

case studies in this chapter, and this shows great promise for systems change in the future.

References

Adisa, O., Allen, K., Kumari, M., Weir, R., & Bond, E. (2020). *Mapping the VAWG funding ecosystem in England and Wales.* Project Report. Centre for Abuse Research, SISER.

Adisa, O., Allen, K., Manning, M., Ferreira, J., & Horvath, M. (2023a). *Drive systems change evaluation: Final report.* Institute for Social Justice and Crime, University of Suffolk.

Adisa, O., James, S., & Newman, D. (2023b). Rural access to justice and beyond: Dimensions of access as a criterion for understanding lay users' satisfaction with remote justice. In *Access to justice in rural communities. Global perspectives.* Bloomsbury.

Adisa, O., & Khan, R. (2021). *The story of H.O.P.E. How a group of Black and Brown women reshaped domestic abuse support networks in lockdown.* Domestic Abuse Research Network (DARNet), University of Suffolk & Honour Abuse Research Matrix (HARM), University of Central Lancashire.

Adisa, O., Maitra, D., Allen, K., Tyrrell, K., & Barbin, A. (2022). *HOPE cross-cultural training evaluation.* University of Suffolk.

Allen K., Hermolle, M., & Adisa, O. (2023). *Embedding knowledge & promoting meaningful change: Evaluating the H.O.P.E 2022–3 Cross-Cultural Training webinars.* Final briefing. University of Suffolk

Back, L. (2021). Hope's work. *Antipode, 53,* 3–20. https://doi.org/10.1111/anti.12644

Bakhtin, M. M. (1986). *Methodology for the human sciences. Speech genres and other late essays* (Emerson, C., & Holquist, M., Eds., V. W. McGee, Trans., pp. 159–172). University of Texas Press.

Casey, L. (2023). *An independent review into the standards of behaviour and internal culture of the Metropolitan Police Service.* https://www.met.police.uk/police-forces/metropolitan-police/areas/about-us/about-the-met/bcr/baroness-casey-review/

Coleman, R., & Ferreday, D. (2010). Introduction: Hope and feminist theory. *Journal for Cultural Research, 14*(4), 313–321.

Collins, P. H. (2022). *Black feminist thought: Knowledge, consciousness, and the politics of empowerment*. Routledge.

Crenshaw, K. (1989). Demarginalizing the intersection of race and sex: A Black feminist critique of antidiscrimination doctrine, feminist theory and antiracist politics. *University of Chicago Legal Forum, 1*(8). https://archive. org/stream/DemarginalizingTheIntersectionOfRaceAndSexABlackFeminis/ Demarginalizing+the+Intersection+of+Race+and+Sex_+A+Black+Feminis_ djvu.txt

Equality Act 2010. London. https://www.legislation.gov.uk/ukpga/2010/15

Foster-Fishman, P. G., & Behrens, T. R. (2007). Systems

Geronimus, A. T. (2023). *Weathering: The extraordinary stress of ordinary life in an unjust society*. Hachette UK.

Government Office for Science. (2023). *Systems Leadership Guide: How to be a systems leader*. https://www.gov.uk/government/publications/systems-leader ship-guide-for-civil-servants/systems-leadership-guide-how-to-be-a-systems-leader

Khan, R., Kumari, M., & Adisa, O. (2020). *Home Secretary—Open Letter: Hidden harm summit for domestic abuse 21 May 2020 COVID-19 impact*. Discussion Paper. UCLan, UK.

hooks, b. (2003). *Teaching community: A pedagogy of hope*. Routledge.

Hopkins, D., & Higham, R. (2007). System leadership: Mapping the landscape. *School Leadership and Management, 27*(2), 147–166.

Imkaan. (2018). *From survival to sustainability*. https://www.imkaan.org.uk/res ources

Kalina, P. (2020). Performative allyship. *Technium Social Science Journal, 11*, 478.

Larasi, M. (2016). A fuss about nothing?: Delivering services to Black and minority ethnic survivors of gender violence—The role of the specialist Black and minority ethnic women's sector. In *Moving in the shadows* (pp. 267–282). Routledge.

Levinas, E. (1978). *Existence and existents* (A. Lingis, Trans.). Nijhoff.

Penchansky, R., & Thomas, J. W. (1981). The concept of access: definition and relationship to consumer satisfaction. *Medical Care, 19*, 127–140.

Rape Crisis England and Wales. (2021). *Women's sector CEOs share statement of support for VAWG Anti-Racism Charter*. https://rapecrisis.org.uk/news/wom ens-sector-ceos-share-statement-of-support-for-vawg-anti-racism-charter/? utm_source=Website&utm_medium=Twitter&utm_campaign=anti-racism

Raynor, R. (2021). Hopes multiplied amidst decline: Understanding gendered precarity in times of austerity. *Environment and Planning D: Society and Space, 39*(3), 553–570.

Safelives. (2023). *End of Year stocktake.* https://safelives.org.uk/EEDI/2021-22

Snyder, C. R. (1994). *The psychology' of hope: You can get there from here.* The Free Press.

Snyder, C. R. (Ed.). (2000). *Handbook of hope: Theory, measures, and applications.* Academic Press.

Stroh, D. P. (2015). *Systems thinking for social change: A practical guide to solving complex problems, avoiding unintended consequences, and achieving lasting results.* Chelsea Green Publishing.

Webb, D. (2007). Modes of hoping. *History of the Human Sciences, 20*(3), 65–83.

Wellman, M. L. (2022). Black squares for Black lives? Performative allyship as credibility maintenance for social media influencers on Instagram. *Social Media+ Society, 8*(1). https://doi.org/10.1177/20563051221080473.

Transforming Consciousness to Change Systems: Deploying Critical Systems Thinking to Enhance Rape Crisis Centre Training

Katherine Allen

Introduction

Sexual violence (SV) is a complex, intransigent and apparently 'wicked' problem, with deep economic, social and cultural roots. In other words, SV can reasonably be characterised as a systemic issue. Accordingly, it is plausible that researchers, practitioners and advocates working in SV can benefit from becoming conversant in critical systems thinking. In this chapter, I discuss how this could potentially be applied, sharing my reflections on the potentialities of systems thinking within the context of SV. This chapter details my exploratory journey of revisiting data from an earlier research project via the lens of critical systems thinking, contributing to this book's purpose of exploring the concept of systems and systems change in relation to gender-based violence. The chapter will specifically explore how Critical Systems Heuristics (CSH) could be used to enhance the development and delivery of volunteer training carried

K. Allen (✉)
University of Suffolk, Suffolk, UK
e-mail: k.allen3@uos.ac.uk

O. Adisa and E. Bond (eds.), *Tackling Domestic Abuse and Sexual Violence*, Palgrave Studies in Victims and Victimology, https://doi.org/10.1007/978-3-031-58600-2_6

out as part of a wider programme of work by Rape Crisis Centres. I argue that CSH could be implemented in the planning, development and implementation of volunteer training, providing a structured approach for surfacing tensions and areas of contestation.

Story of the Research

The interviews discussed in this chapter were undertaken in 2019 for a research project exploring Rape Crisis Centre (RCC) workers' perceptions in relation to their volunteer training.

The research was conducted from an insider standpoint, drawing on my own perspective as a worker at 'Home Centre' and my links with both Home and 'Sister Centre'.

As part of my induction as a RCC helpline volunteer, I had completed specialist training developed by Rape Crisis England and Wales (RCEW). The experience of completing this training was the genesis for the research. I experienced the training programme as akin to a form of consciousness-raising (CR), enabling trainees to collectively consider and interrogate prevailing ways of thinking (and not thinking) about the societal prevalence and distribution of SV. This centrally included the articulation of SV as a cause and consequence of gender inequality, as well as discussions about our own experiences of gendered discrimination and sexual violence—including 'everyday' intrusions such as sexual harassment in public spaces and the dismissive or punitive responses from those around us—and societal responses to perpetration.

Starting from the assumption that this course represented a standardised programme of study across RCCs in England and Wales, I sought to explore how women working in two English RCCs responded to key concepts referenced as part of the training, namely a feminist account of SV as a systemic social and political issue and the overarching vision of ending SV. The semi-structured interview schedules were designed to examine how participants experienced the feminist account of SV during their initial training and subsequent RCC work, and whether the training served, like CR speak-outs, as a means of 'connecting the dots' between the personal and political.

At the time of the research, Sister Centre was a well-established RCC which had been supporting women via its helpline since the early 1980s. Like many RCCs, Sister Centre honoured its radical feminist roots while having transitioned to a more professionalised organisational structure. During volunteer training, the predominant focus was on practice rather than theory, with the training process primarily operating to outline, and instil, the core knowledge and competencies needed for supporting survivors.

Home Centre was a newer RCC which emerged as a fledgling, helpline-only service in 2010. Like Sister Centre, it remained committed to the radical principles of the early Rape Crisis movement. As with Sister Centre, it had a professionalised organisational structure. In contrast to Sister Centre, the volunteer training sessions incorporated explicit discussion of the systemic nature of SV, with early sessions including exercises designed to prompt reflection on how SV is caused by and contributes to gender inequality.

The nine interview participants were diverse in age, sexual orientation and disability status. Eight identified as White British, with one participant identifying as White Mixed, a finding which reflects regional demographic trends but could also speak to the potential for survivorship bias when recruiting interviewees who completed the training and remain involved with the Rape Crisis movement.

This chapter revisits these interview findings, reflecting on them through a systems lens. I argue that Critical Systems Heuristics (CSH) (Ulrich, 1983) could provide a framework for developing and enriching training programmes for incoming RCC volunteers, flagging areas of tension within (and beyond) the feminist movement and local interested parties and beneficiaries. Equally, it could highlight neglected perspectives that could be 'swept in' to create a more representative and transformative programme that serves the interests of a wider range of victim-survivors and communities[1] (Churchman, 1968).

---

[1] Epistemic marginalisation or injustice can take multiple forms and has been differently theorised by various feminist scholars. For the purposes of my original study, I applied Fricker's (2007) definition of epistemic injustice, which encompasses both hermeneutical (interpretive) and testimonial (perceived credibility) elements and which constitutively affects societally marginalised groups.

'The Art of Discovery'[2]: Introducing CSH and Feminist Epistemologies

Systems thinking is a theoretically diverse and methodologically pluralist family of approaches

CSH is a framework within this tradition which centrally involves the use of boundary critique; a reflective process organised around a series of 12 questions designed to clarify our beliefs and values about what (and who) matters within a given 'system of concern', particularly in relation to motivation, control, expertise and legitimacy (Ulrich, 1996, p. 17). CSH lays out a pathway for deliberation, designed to equip participants to competently take part in planning 'improvement by and for the people' (Ulrich, 1996, p. 15). Ultimately, the aim of CSH is to 'give people a voice in matters that are important to them', contesting elite institutional monopolies of knowledge and power and empowering citizens to become '"experts" of their own lives' (Ulrich, 1996, p. 6). In some important respects, this dialogical and democratising mode of knowledge production parallels the role of CR during the Women's Liberation Movement (WLM).

One of the major achievements of the twentieth-century WLM was the cultivation of a shared vocabulary that enabled women to name previously 'unspeakable' experiences such as sexual harassment and marital rape and, just as importantly, to identify them as 'ideological and political rather than isolated and personal' (Kelland, 2016, p. 733). Through CR speak-outs, women were able to join the dots between individual experiences of victimisation or oppression, perceiving that they were just 'one among many' (Bartky, 1975, p. 431).

Grassroots CR groups developed as a form of feminist praxis in the late 1960s–early 1970s, transforming individual stirrings of discontent into collective 'grievances' (MacKinnon, 1989, p. 86). Through collectively articulating and reframing experiences of gendered oppression, participants were able to develop 'a radically altered consciousness' of themselves, others and the social world (Bartky, 1975, p. 426). CR

---

[2] Ulrich (2005, p. 1).

presented both 'a method for arriving at the truth and a means for action and organizing' (Sarachild, 1978, p. 147).

In relation to SV, this broad patterning of experiences suggested that rape was not, as had previously been believed, rare, anomalous and essentially apolitical, but was both common and continuous with 'a particular socially-constructed version of maleness' (Jones & Cook, 2008, pp. 5–6). This construction of SV opened up new pathways for addressing perpetration. Specifically, through linking what had been perceived as abhorrent, but essentially private, acts to unjust societal conditions, feminist theorists brought focus to the ways in which oppressive and/or dysfunctional social institutions create a conducive context for sexual violence.

As this summary suggests, there are clear affinities between critical systems thinking and the epistemic techniques and frameworks developed and employed by grassroots feminists and elaborated by feminists working at the frontline of social justice movements and/or in academia. These parallels include:

- A foundational concern for positionality and power relations, and a rejection of naively positivistic understandings of knowledge construction. Knowledge claims are socially situated, and, as such, feminist thinkers are sceptical of those who claim to be presenting a 'view from nowhere' (Harding, 1995). Rather, those who occupy societally marginalised standpoints have a distinctive 'angle of vision' (Hill Collins, 2022, p. 138).
- The interrogation of settled and unspoken assumptions about what is salient (and whose perspectives should be taken into account). CR groups gave extended focus to everyday issues such as reproductive health, domestic labour and sexuality which were frequently dismissed by the wider Left movement as 'therapeutic' concerns beyond or beneath political scrutiny (Hanisch, 2006). By providing a forum for women to discuss these issues, CR disclosed the political dimensions of private life and the epistemic value of women's lived experiences.
- A distinctively ethical process which supports coalition-building, collaborative meaning-making and social transformation. Early CR

groups were founded on an ethic of 'openness, honesty and self-awareness' (MacKinnon, 1989, p. 85) and tended to operate informally and non-hierarchically, without rules, methodology or conventional markers of expertise (Sarachild, 1978). CR groups were not just theory- but action-generating, designed 'to get to the most radical truths about the situation of women in order to take radical action' (ibid., p. 149).

There are also notable points of departure. According to contemporaneous accounts, grassroots CR groups enabled women to identify salient commonalities, relating aspects of their personal experience to the 'general condition of women', with the aim not of rejecting generalisations but producing 'truer ones' (Sarachild, 1978, p. 145). While recognising that race and class shaped women's experiences, prominent radical feminist theorists argued that CR revealed that 'simply being a woman has a meaning that decisively defines all women socially' (MacKinnon, 1989, p. 90). Meanwhile, CSH is engineered to surface contrasting viewpoints and explore the tensions between these (Ulrich & Reynolds, 2020). Both approaches are ultimately action-focused and oriented towards systems change, but CSH represents a systematic and structured process, while CR speak-outs emerged more organically as part of radical feminist praxis (Sarachild, 1978).

Perhaps owing to these differences, despite the shared concerns and tendencies discussed above, until relatively recently 'gender specific or feminist research [was] very nearly absent in systems theory' (Stephens et al., 2010, p. 555). The assertion that there has been a lack of specifically 'feminist research' in systems theory should be understood as a path-dependent or contingent claim rather than a statement of incompatibility—linked to an historic association between systems theory and formative theorists whose work was perceived as positivist and conservative (Hanson, 2001; Stephens et al., 2010). Equally, it is important to note that this claim relates to formalised, academic applications of systems approaches, rather than broadly 'systemic' thinking, which has arguably been employed by Black and minoritised feminists dating back to the Combahee River Collective statement (1977) and before.

Equally, as this chapter will discuss, feminist mobilisations such as the Rape Crisis movement are intrinsically 'systemic' in intent and scope, seeking to transform unjust social institutions. While volunteer training and the tensions between grassroots feminist and professionalised/'bureaucratic' perspectives have previously been explored through a critical systems lens (see Cohen, 1996), this chapter is the first, to our knowledge, to explore the applicability of CSH to Rape Crisis volunteer training.

This chapter argues that CSH techniques could represent a particularly useful tool for those working within volunteer/staff training and development within Rape Crisis Centres in England and Wales.

The Rape Crisis Movement, Rape Crisis Centres and Training Interventions

Rape Crisis Centres (RCCs) emerged as part of a wider epistemic and political project, born of grassroots feminist activism. From their inception, RCCs were designed to support victim-survivors and mobilise efforts for social and political change, working not just to ameliorate but to end sexual violence. Early RCCs aimed to embody their egalitarian values through collective and non-hierarchical organisational models and were often staffed by volunteers rather than professionals (Jones & Cook, 2008). There was a wave of professionalisation and 'insider drift' (MacKay, 2013, p. 272) in British RCCs throughout the 1990s, with centres reporting pressure to deemphasise or relinquish some of their more challenging ideals and working practices in order to appease the funders financing vital frontline services.

In spite of this shift from an overtly activist, grassroots organisational model to an increasing focus on service provision, RCEW still works from a feminist perspective that recognises sexual violence as a cause and consequence of gender inequality. RCCs provide services but are not (or are not only) service providers; while they support and counsel individual victim-survivors, they continue to make up part of a wider movement to transform society. However, while RCEW-affiliated centres share core aims and perspectives there are not-insignificant variations in philosophy and practice between RCCs; the Rape Crisis movement more closely resembles a loose assemblage of principles and commitments than a 'franchise operation replicated over a number of locations' (Jones & Cook, 2008, p. 38).

The wider literature on RCCs in England and Wales suggests that provision for incoming volunteers forms part of the distinctive 'living dynamic' of RCCs (Jones & Cook, 2008, p. 50). For some participants, the training acts as a form of 'facilitated consciousness-raising', as well as an introduction to the practical skills and knowledge needed for the volunteer work, although pragmatic considerations have resulted in a drift towards shorter training courses (ibid.).

The same body of literature suggests that volunteer training across centres demonstrates a degree of 'convergent evolution' given the common work with which volunteers are tasked, but that centres enjoy a degree of flexibility that enables them to adapt to local contexts and accommodate the needs of their service users (Rath, 2008, p. 6).

RCC Training and Feminist Consciousness: Returning to Selected Findings from the Original Study

The following section elucidates two of the key findings from my original study; firstly, the variations between and within centres in relation to the content and format of the training—specifically in relation to the centrality/marginality of CR-like discussions about SV and gendered oppression—and secondly regarding the perspectives of participants affected by interlocking forms of marginalisation.

After detailing these findings, I argue that the points of tension or dysfluency they disclose suggest areas where CSH could be used to improve RCC training and recruitment processes. I argue that CSH could be utilised both prior to/during planning stages by trainers and other interested parties (ensuring that a wide range of community members are'in the room' to begin with), and iteratively during the programme itself.

Revisiting RCC Research Findings

Marginality of Exploratory/CR-Like Discussion

Interview findings underlined that training varies considerably between and within centres. Training may be affected by a number of contextual factors such as staff availability, group size and scheduling, in addition to more substantive differences in philosophy or pedagogy between trainers and centres.

Strikingly, just two of the nine participants (both from Home Centre) had received training explicitly advancing a feminist account of SV as a cause and consequence of gender inequality, which had formed a core aspect of my own volunteer training. Moreover, while some participants such as Sarah,[3] who had trained as part of a smaller cohort, felt that they had the chance to engage in more exploratory discussions 'around' the primary training materials, others, such as Danielle, felt that their training was necessarily more practical in orientation, limiting the scope for and appropriateness of, wider-ranging discussions:

> I think one of the things that was really clear from the training is "**We're gonna tell you and teach you these things because this is what you need to do the helpline**", rather than it being kind of a general academic or even a kind of experiential discussion group around feminism and patriarchy and gender inequality

This finding problematises the assumption that contemporary RCC training takes facilitating CR-like discussions or initiating volunteers into the wider Rape Crisis movement, as one of its constitutive aims.

LBT Women

Thematic analysis of the nine interviews also highlighted 'experiences at the intersections'; areas where RCC training content and/or delivery

---

[3] All participants were assigned pseudonyms to protect their confidentiality, which are used in this chapter when participants are referred to by 'name'.

context was an uneasy fit for participants whose needs and lived experiences are shaped by interconnecting forms of marginalisation.

Notably, there were interpretive gaps and misalignments between the feminist account of SV and participants' lived experience.

For example, one bisexual participant, Ella, found the feminist account of SV illuminating and 'validating' when thinking about SV at a societal level, and in relation to her experiences of men's stranger intrusions. However, it offered less clarity when making sense of violence perpetrated by a female ex-partner.

> What I did find a limitation…to begin with, was that I'm very open in that I have experienced sexual abuse, although obviously I wouldn't go as far to use the word rape, purely because it has been from a female partner. And…**I've very much struggled with that for a long time within the feminist sphere, because that's definitely something that's not talked about, um…and, so that was very, that was a very isolating experience for me.**

As Ella observed, the focus on SV as a gendered phenomenon is, in one sense, reasonable and proportionate in light of the statistics which demonstrate it to be overwhelmingly male-perpetrated. However, for those women who have been abused by female perpetrators, it is plausible that a feminist account of SV could compound the epistemic harms already associated with being subjected to SV unless sufficient attention is paid to explicating the ways in which a minority of women also become complicit in, or choose to enact, gendered violence in a male-dominated and sexually-violent society.

This issue may be particularly acute for lesbian, bisexual and trans women working within the Rape Crisis movement, with potential knock-on effects for equitable recruitment, retention, service provision and advocacy. Gender-based violence that occurs within the context of LGBT+ communities and relationships is often perceived to 'sit outside of a predominantly heteronormative, cisnormative, feminist, social-structural analysis', leaving victim-survivors to account for their experiences through other available explanatory frameworks, including narratives of individual aberrance or psychopathology (Donovan & Barnes, 2020, p. 555).

Disability and Class

While generally characterising the training environment as a safe and welcoming space, one participant, Bryony, noted that her memories of the volunteer training were heavily coloured by accessibility issues she had encountered while attending:

> I have a sleep disorder so ((laughs)) actually getting here for ten in the morning I found really hard, **but I didn't tell them because I didn't want to be difficult about it, I would just make myself do it**. So, you know, I would feel like a zombie for the entire day of the training and then I would suffer for like at least a day or so afterwards. But it was my choice to do that, I felt like it was worth it to do something worthwhile.

While generally highly positive about the Centre and staff members, Bryony remained hesitant to communicate her experiences of feeling marginalised in relation to her disability:

> So yeah that is disabling, but it's a difficult thing to challenge because people still have this idea that disabilities are visible [i.e. wheelchair users...] but an invisible disability where, okay, you can do the thing, it's just harder, rather than you actually, physically 100% can't...People just don't view it the same way.

Bryony was additionally the only participant to raise socioeconomic class as a factor in her experience of the training. When asked about aspects of the training she had found challenging, she noted that initially entering the training room as a woman from a working-class background had proved daunting:

> I suppose I felt like I didn't fit in particularly well with the other people here, but that's not their fault ((laughs)) that's my fault, I'd only recently moved to [Town] and I remember joking to my husband before the first

session, I was like: 'I bet I'll go there, and they'll all have PhDs, and they'll all be brilliant and glamorous and so on'. ((laughs)) And they did all have PhDs and they were all glamorous ((laughs)) […] and, yeah, I suppose I felt a bit inferior, but they didn't make me feel that way. That's me, with my baggage, like no one said, 'you're working-class, fuck off', you know? ((laughs)) […] You kind of expect to be stigmatised and looked down on and so on. And the people were really inclusive, they were fine, but it just was a bit intimidating.

The conspicuous absence of (visibly) similarly-situated trainees—identifiably working-class women without 'glamorous' lifestyles or prestigious careers—was felt as intimidating, perhaps particularly when encountered within the context of a deeply 'classed' society in which signifiers such as accent and clothes retain an 'immediate discursive impact' (Fricker, 2007, p. 261).

Relevantly, Bryony observed that requesting professional and personal references from prospective volunteers might prove exclusionary, deterring those with less social capital from applying:

If you're working-class you probably don't know someone that sounds impressive ((laughs)) to put down on the thing. You know, you might have a zero-hours contract, you're more likely to have a shitty job where, like, people aren't going to stick up for you.

Bryony felt that this was '*fundamentally really disempowering*', putting women into the position of relying on socially imposing 'others' to speak about and for them. Such a requirement might be seen to reflect both positive and negative aspects of RCEW's increasing professionalisation, increasing accountability via the development of consistent policies and procedures but potentially erecting further barriers to participation for some women.

Re-viewing Through a Systems Lens

Ulrich's 12 CSH questions provide a structured framework for making boundary judgements visible and exploring their implications for different stakeholders, with the ultimate aim of determining *what constitutes an improvement for this grouping of people, within this system of concern* (Ulrich, 1996). Each question relates to a central boundary 'category' in both a normative and a descriptive mode: for example, who (and what ends) should the system be serving, and whose interests and which purposes is it actually serving at present.

If we take RCC volunteer training as our system of concern, it becomes apparent how applying just two[4] of the normative or 'ought' questions from Ulrich's CSH framework may help to surface underlying assumptions and values and trace their implications:

1. What should be the purpose or outcomes of the training?
2. Whose interests should the training serve?

Without taking for granted that volunteer training *should* act as a site of feminist CR, an explicit, structured examination of *who* and *what* we consider the training is ultimately for may help to surface and adjudicate between differing perspectives on the evolving structure and role of RCCs, with implications for volunteer recruitment and training processes. As noted, despite the convergence of different RCC training programmes regarding core themes, there are still discrepancies between and within centres in relation to content and experiential quality, including the extent to which trainees themselves perceive exploratory discussions about gendered oppression and social justice as 'within scope'. These may reflect underlying differences in how volunteers, staff, service users, community members and decision-makers across RCCs conceive of the parameters of their/their centre's role as part of a wider movement against SV.

---

[4] Due to limited space, this chapter cannot do justice to each of the 12 CSH questions, but it is hoped that the two featured 'ought' questions provide some indication of the scope for application.

If I understand the purpose of training to be equipping trainees with the immediate knowledge and skills needed to support victim-survivors who access the service, I may be more likely to regard CR-like explorations of feminism(s) and gender-based violence as tangential or discretionary. Meanwhile, if I take an expansive view of RCC volunteers as part of a social justice movement, I may instead assume that volunteer training should empower trainees to critically engage with the assumptions and values undergirding the Rape Crisis movement and to confront systemic dysfunctionalities and inequality. What such an approach would look like in concrete terms may vary based on the systemic issues facing victim-survivors at this time and/or place. For example, in rural areas this may include working to address limited access to specialist services, while at a national level, this could involve mobilising against policies which criminalise victim-survivors with irregular/uncertain immigration status.

Equally, when looking at issues of marginalisation, if I operate from the uninterrogated assumption that the primary (or rightful) beneficiaries of my local RCC's activities are:

- cisgender female victim-survivors of male-perpetrated SV
- who have experienced unambiguously criminalised forms of SV
- who are living locally and can give a fixed address/consistent contact details
- who have chosen to seek formal support
- who have chosen to make contact with the RCC via 'approved' channels and are seen to communicate in legible, socially 'appropriate' ways with professionals/fellow service users
- who feel comfortable and able to access support from the RCC through its existing services

I am likely to operate with a more constrained sense of remit for training/recruitment than if I take the intended beneficiaries to be all local women and girls affected by any form of SV. Operating with this broader understanding, I might expect those coordinating volunteer training/recruitment to be highly attentive to questions of accessibility and representation, with the aim of building a RCC workforce capable of meeting the needs and advancing the interests, of a range of victim-survivors.

Such an approach might include exploring whether institutional training/recruitment processes counteract, or reproduce, discriminatory social norms, asking:

- Do existing recruitment and training processes work to welcome in, or to gatekeep, women affected by intersecting forms of marginalisation?
- Do they create an environment which fosters explicit and psychologically safe discussion of power and privilege? Is training content and delivery premised on unexamined assumptions about those who need and use RCC services—do volunteers receive training which highlights the experiences of a range of victim-survivors, including Black, Asian and minoritised, migrant, LBT, working class and disabled women and women subject to multiple disadvantage?

Initiating these counterfactual 'discussions' in the context of my study findings is not intended to suggest that planning for volunteer training/recruitment at either centre was undertaken without consideration of inclusion, or that decision-makers were operating from narrow boundary judgements regarding the purposes and beneficiaries of RCCs. As previously noted, both centres remained committed to feminist principles and meeting the needs of victim-survivors, while most interviewees highly valued their learning experiences from the training.

Rather—to proceed by analogy—just as contemporary writers in the WLM critiqued the prevalence of unstructured groups, on the grounds that apparent 'structurelessness' typically masks informal (and therefore unaccountable) power dynamics and divisions of labour (Freeman, 1972), unarticulated boundary judgements may exert a more insidious influence than those which have been explicitly critiqued. Employing CSH to surface assumptions and values enables participants to reveal sites of contestation or confusion, including areas where values conflict or are ill-served by existing practice.

Conclusion

When revisiting these findings, I chose to highlight these particular interview fragments as snapshots into interviewees' experiences, which highlight why CSH frameworks could be beneficial for creating a more inclusive, ambitious and transformative RCC curriculum and training environment. In turn, by designing the initial volunteer induction and training process in a participatory and transparent manner, RCCs can create a more equitable environment for minoritised and marginalised workers and service users.

As discussed in previous sections, while RCEW-affiliated centres share core values in relation to promoting gender equality, challenging societal tolerance of SV and empowering victim-survivors, RCCs do not work from a uniform training programme. Individual centres therefore have a reasonable degree of latitude in how they respond to local contexts. By utilising structured boundary questions with a range of interested parties, RCCs can forge a more transparent and dialogical approach to programme development. To mitigate issues regarding sampling or survivorship bias, which may compound existing trends of underrepresentation and epistemic marginalisation, this consultative process should not be limited to those who are already viewed as RCC experts or 'insiders'. Where practical and ethically appropriate, programme developers should seek to engage a wide range of community members.

By making explicit the boundary judgements within which different parties are operating, programme developers and their interlocuters can identify and negotiate tensions; for example, delineating what constitutes relevant skills and knowledge and the extent to which the assumptive use of 'respectable' referees as a guarantor could disproportionately disadvantage working-class and marginalised women seeking to volunteer with the Rape Crisis movement. Equally, dialogical exploration and interrogation of feminist accounts of SV with a diverse range of interlocutors could pinpoint differences in interpretation and worldview which may impact perceived legitimacy and personal salience, with knock-on effects for volunteer recruitment/retainment.

Key Points

- Grassroots CR discussions emerged as a form of feminist praxis in the late 1960s–early 1970s WLM.
- Through these discussions, participants articulated SV as a prevalent and politically salient, issue facing women and girls, which was linked to systemic gender inequality.
- The global Rape Crisis movement emerged from grassroots organising against SV. While RCCs became increasingly professionalised during the 1990s onwards, RCEW-affiliated centres in England and Wales remain feminist and socially engaged, with wider political commitments in addition to service provision.
- CSH was developed by critical systems thinker Werner Ulrich to facilitate 'boundary critique', a process of unfolding and critically engaging with alternative assumptions and values underlying different plans for improvement (Ulrich, 1983).
- CSH centrally focuses on questions relating to motivation, control, expertise and legitimacy, operating in a descriptive and a normative mode.
- CSH shares parallels with grassroots CR discussions, but affords a systematic approach for surfacing relevant boundary judgements which may be left unarticulated/uninterrogated during less structured discussions.
- Selected findings from my research with RCC workers point to areas of potential conflict between current volunteer training and recruitment practices and the needs and experiences of some marginalised women.
- RCCs should review and revise training and induction processes on an ongoing basis in negotiation with local interested parties.
- This should be a meaningfully participatory process, employing CSH techniques to systematically surface and critique contrasting viewpoints and explore how these can be negotiated.

References

Bartky, S. L. (1975). Toward a phenomenology of feminist consciousness. *Social Theory and Practice, 3*(4), 425–439.

Churchman, C. W. (1968). *Challenge to reason.* McGraw-Hill.

Cohen, C. (1996). Two perspectives in a voluntary organization. In *Critical systems thinking: Current research and practice* (pp. 235–250). Springer.

The Combahee River Collective. (1977). *The Combahee River Collective statement.* https://rapereliefshelter.bc.ca/the-combahee-river-collective-statement/

Donovan, C., & Barnes, R. (2020). Help-seeking among lesbian, gay, bisexual and/or transgender victims/survivors of domestic violence and abuse: The impacts of cisgendered heteronormativity and invisibility. *Journal of Sociology, 56*(4), 554–570.

Freeman, J. (1972). The tyranny of structurelessness. *Berkeley Journal of Sociology, 17*, 151–164.

Fricker, M. (2007). *Epistemic injustice: Power and the ethics of knowing.* Oxford University Press.

Hanisch, C. (2006) *The personal is political: The women's liberation classic with a new explanatory introduction.* Available at: https://www.carolhanisch.org/CHwritings/PIP.html. (Accessed on 31 May 2024).

Hanson, B. (2001). Systems theory and the spirit of feminism: Grounds for a connection. *Systems Research and Behavioral Science, 18*(6), 545–556.

Harding, S. (1995). "Strong objectivity": A response to the new objectivity question. *Synthese, 104*(3), 331–349. https://doi.org/10.1007/BF01064504

Hill Collins, P. (2022). *Black feminist thought 30th Anniversary Edition: Knowledge, consciousness, and the politics of empowerment.* Routledge.

Jones, H., & Cook, K. (2008). *Rape crisis: Responding to sexual violence.* Russell House Publishing.

Kelland, L. (2016). A call to arms: The centrality of feminist consciousness-raising speak-outs to the recovery of rape survivors. *Hypatia, 31*(4), 730–745.

Mackay, F. (2013). *The march of reclaim the night: Feminist activism in movement.* (Doctoral dissertation, University of Bristol).

MacKinnon, C. A. (1989). *Towards a feminist theory of the state.* Harvard University Press.

Rath, J. (2008). Training to be a volunteer Rape Crisis counsellor: A qualitative study of women's experiences. *British Journal of Guidance & Counselling, 36*(1), 19–32.

Sarachild, K. (1978). *Consciousness raising: a radical weapon* (p. 144). NA.

Stephens, A., Jacobson, C., & King, C. (2010). Describing a feminist-systems theory. *Systems Research and Behavioral Science, 27*(5), 553–566.

Ulrich, W. (1983). *Critical heuristics of social planning: A new approach to practical philosophy.* Wiley.

Ulrich, W. (1996). *A primer to critical systems heuristics for action researchers.* Centre for Systems Studies.

Ulrich, W. (2005). *A brief introduction to critical systems heuristics (CSH).* ECOSENSUS Project Site. https://citeseerx.ist.psu.edu/document?repid=rep1&type=pdf&doi=3fe2510b58a3f9e9a4939ae9d3416c1e5c556c8f

Ulrich, W., & Reynolds, M. (2020). Critical systems heuristics: The idea and practice of boundary critique. *Systems Approaches to Making Change: A Practical Guide,* 255–306.

Other Institutional Responses
and Applications of Systems Approaches

A Systems Approach to Preventing and Responding to Abusive Image Sharing Among Young People

Emily Setty

Introduction

Sexual image sharing among young people, commonly referred to as 'youth produced sexual imagery' (YPSI), has been identified as a potentially developmentally normative way that young people flirt, build intimacy, and express themselves in the 'digital age' (McGeeney & Hanson, 2017; Scott et al., 2020), but also as involving acts of abuse (Ringrose et al., 2021). What has been termed 'image-based sexual abuse' (IBSA) refers to the non-consensual further distribution of images (McGlynn & Rackley, 2017), while 'technology-facilitated sexual violence' (TFSV) also includes unwanted solicitation for images and pressure to produce images, sending unwanted images ('cyber-flashing' or 'unsolicited dick pics'), faked or non-consensually recorded or produced images (e.g., 'upskirting'), and coercion to produce images and threats to release images ('sextortion') (Henry et al., 2018; Ringrose et al., 2021; Setty

E. Setty (✉)
University of Surrey, Guildford, UK
e-mail: emily.setty@surrey.ac.uk

© The Author(s), under exclusive license to Springer Nature
Switzerland AG 2024
O. Adisa and E. Bond (eds.), *Tackling Domestic Abuse and Sexual Violence*, Palgrave
Studies in Victims and Victimology, https://doi.org/10.1007/978-3-031-58600-2_7

et al., 2022; Wolak et al., 2018). These behaviours are, seemingly, pervasive and normalised among young people. The current scale of problem was made evident in testimonials shared by young people to the 'Everyone's Invited' Instagram page and website, which, at the time of writing, has accrued over 54,000 stories of peer-to-peer sexual violence, abuse, and harassment taking place in schools in England. A 'rapid review' subsequently conducted by Ofsted called for urgent action to prevent and respond to incidents, including of IBSA and TFSV (Ofsted, 2021).

In this chapter, I discuss the need for a systems response to preventing and responding to all forms of abusive image sharing which holistically tackles the underlying causes of abuse and the barriers to reporting and challenging abuse that exist both within peer culture and the structures of the systems themselves (Lloyd, 2019). As Churchman (1968) first argued, a system may seemingly have a logic but does not operate apart from its context and of those within it. This chapter takes a 'soft' critical systems approach that is concerned with social rather than objective components (Checkland & Poulter, 2020) and centres the beliefs and values that drive a system and that may hinder its effectiveness (Reynolds, 2011). Applied to the prevention and response to YPSI, it requires *surfacing* 'adultist' (Phippen & Street, 2022) beliefs about the nature of the problem and the goals for and means of solving the problem and re-orienting to protection from harm (Phippen & Bond, 2023) and to addressing the social inequalities that shape the perpetration and experience of harm, for example, regarding gender (Setty et al., 2022).

I start by describing the educational and criminal justice policy and practice context regarding YPSI. Drawing on a recently completed study about the impacts of lockdown on young people's relationships, I then outline the sociocultural contexts that shape abusive image sharing among young people. I finish by offering suggestions for an improved systems approach.

Educational and Criminal Justice Policy and Practice on YPSI

There have been several developments in educational and criminal justice policy and practice on YPSI. Yet, there remain tensions in the aims and nature of the approach which means that barriers to preventing, reporting, and responding to abusive image sharing have not been fully resolved. From the outset of the emergence of YPSI as a phenomenon, existing laws in England pertaining to the production, storage, and distribution of illicit imagery of minors (see the Sexual Offences Act 2003, s45[1]) have been used to deter YPSI and to (formally or informally) punish those who share images (see Moran-Ellis, 2012). The rationale for doing so relates to a framing of YPSI as self-exploitation and, in turn, the state's obligation to protect young people through deterring them from sharing images (see Guice, 2015; Leary, 2008). Over time, however, the counterproductive and harmful impacts of criminalising (or threatening the criminalisation of) young people for YPSI have increasingly been recognised, including, as outlined below, by criminal justice agencies, as well as academics in the field (Lee et al., 2015). These impacts include the stigma of criminalisation and the barriers to reporting abuse due to fears of self-incrimination among victim-survivors.

This shift in outlook is evident in police and Crown Prosecution Service (CPS) guidance. The former has implemented a system of recording all incidents of YPSI that are identified by or reported to the police but with an option of 'Outcome 21' (essentially, 'no further action') where the incident does not involve any aggravated or abusive elements (CoP, 2016; NPCC, 2016a) and the CPS has stated that it is unlikely to be in the public to prosecute cases of YPSI unless aggravated or abusive (CPS, 2018).Safeguarding referrals are to be made as deemed necessary, but the priority is the best interests of the child, with the aim of avoiding the undue criminalisation of young people involved in consensual image sharing. There is some lack of clarity about whether

---

[1] s45 of the SOA 2003 updated the Protection from Children Act 1978 and the Criminal Justice Act 1988 to include 16- and 17-year-olds under laws prohibiting the "taking, making, permitting to take, distributing, showing, possessing with intent to distribute, and advertising indecent photographs or pseudo-photographs of children".

the police record will appear in a criminal records check (Arthur, 2018; Hales, 2018) although some reassurance that it would only do so in an enhanced check at the discretion of the officer, for example, if it reflected a sustained pattern of behaviour (NPCC, 2016b). Yet, in practice, there has been a diversity of responses between police forces (Bond & Phippen, 2019; Phippen & Bond, 2023).

In line with developing criminal justice policy and practice, the most recent UK Council for Internet Safety guidance to schools on dealing with YPSI (UKCIS, 2020) recommends a proportionate response to incidents that are only to be referred to police if aggravated or abusive. Schools are to act in line with safeguarding duties and, where necessary, refer to police and/or children's social care via the Multi-Agency Safeguarding Hub and to inform the parents of those involved about incidents and action taken (unless deemed unsafe to do so). The guidance also recommends working with bodies like the Internet Watch Foundation (IWF) to remove any images circulated online. Emphasised throughout is the need for a trauma-informed and supportive approach to victim-survivors that does not blame or shame them for abuse and that maintains open lines of communication between pupils and staff to encourage reporting. There are also recommendations for preventative education to tackle the root causes of abuse in terms of consent, respect, and healthy relationships and addressing norms, stereotypes, and bystander roles and responsibilities. Relatedly, the most recent iteration of the NCA-CEOP Thinkuknow educational resource on YPSI designed for use with 11- to 14-year-olds focuses on consent, privacy, and the wider peer culture surrounding image sharing. The police may be involved with such education and have been advised "to work with schools to educate children on the risks of exchanging imagery" (CoP, 2016).

Other relevant national policy, including 'Keeping Children Safe in Education' (DfE, 2022) and 'Sexual harassment and sexual violence between children in schools and colleges' (DfE, 2021, likewise emphasises trauma-informed and contextualised responses to YPSI and outlines a range of statutory and non-statutory bodies that schools should work with to safeguard and support young people involved in abusive image sharing, including the perpetrator. There is also emphasis on identifying the needs of the broader pupil population, including any bullying and harassment that arises from pupils 'taking sides' if an incident becomes public knowledge. These guidance and policy documents instruct schools to take a 'zero tolerance' approach to all forms of sexual violence, abuse, and harassment among pupils, including that related to YPSI, and to deliver preventative education that tackles the underlying causes of the behaviour.

Educating young people about YPSI is part of the now-mandatory Relationships, Sex, and Health Education (RSHE) curriculum for schools in England. Despite the nuanced and contextualised approach recommended in the UKCIS (2020) guidance, Department for Education (DfE) guidance on the curriculum focuses on deterrence through learning objectives pertaining to the illegality of YPSI (Setty & Dobson, 2022). There is no mention of educating about types or contextual causes of abusive image sharing, nor the avenues for reporting and recourse available to victim-survivors. There are broad statements about the need for schools to tackle "everyday sexism, misogyny, homophobia and gender stereotypes and take positive action to build a culture where these not tolerated, and any occurrences are identified and tackled" (DfE 2019, p. 14), yet no specific application of these objectives to YPSI in terms of abusive image sharing, despite, as discussed below, the centrality of these issues to the contextual causes of abuse. There is, therefore, an ongoing problem with the conflation of abusive and non-abusive sharing contrary to the emphasis on protecting young people from undue criminalisation and improving reporting rates, responses to, and prevention of abuse. In response to the above-mentioned Ofsted review, the government is producing new non-statutory guidance 'Teaching Relationships Education to prevent sexual harassment and sexual violence', but it is unclear whether and how abusive image sharing will be addressed.

The Sociocultural Context of Abusive Image Sharing and the Barriers to Reporting and Challenging Abuse

Research with young people suggests YPSI comprises a range of consensual and non-consensual practices and occurs within a wider sociocultural context in which circulations of power, reward, shame, and stigma shape how young people act and treat one another within digitally mediated youth sexual culture (Doyle et al., 2021). YPSI may involve subtle, indirect pressures and expectations as well as direct pressure, force, and coercion (Cooper et al., 2016; García-Gómez, 2017; Ringrose et al., 2012, 2021; Setty, 2020a; Thomas, 2018). Girls are, seemingly, more likely to be victims of abusive shaming and to experience pressure to share images with boys and social shaming for doing so, while boys can accrue social capital, for example, through collecting and sharing images of girls with male peers who enjoy viewing the images and, in turn, reward the boy as a 'lad' for obtaining them (Ringrose et al., 2012, 2021). The evidence also shows that girls often blame themselves for and do not report abusive image sharing perpetrated against them. Boys, meanwhile, are under pressure from, what has been termed, a 'homosocial masculine reward economy' that normalises and celebrates predatory and abusive behaviour, including the collection and distribution of sexual images of girls (Ringrose et al., 2011, 2021; Setty et al., 2022). This context involves images of girls representing something akin to 'tokens' that boys distribute among themselves as a way of performing masculinity, bonding with one another, and gaining social inclusion (Ringrose & Harvey, 2015). It may, however, also entail the shaming of boys who fail to achieve idealised constructs of heterosexual masculinity. Such shaming is typically trivialised by young people as 'banter' yet creates a precarious terrain for boys that facilitates the perpetration of abuse toward them (Ravn et al., 2021; Ringrose & Harvey, 2015; Setty, 2020b; Setty et al., 2022).

These problems were evident in a recent qualitative study that myself and colleague, Emma Dobson, conducted into the impacts of lockdown on relationships for young people (Setty & Dobson, 2022). Some of the girls in the study talked about being sent unsolicited images and pressure to reciprocate both by boys they know and 'strangers' online. Skye (14 F), for example, said that boys and men add them on Snapchat via the "quick add" function and immediately send messages saying "like, 'Hey, do you send?'". Another girl described a pressure to reciprocate based on expectation and obligation (see Setty et al., 2022):

...if they send something... then you feel pressured to send something back or else you just feel a bit weird about it...I don't think it's a direct pressure from people, 'You need to send this', maybe sometimes, but I think a lot of the times it will be them doing it to you first and then it will be like the pressure of them for you.

Emma (16 F), meanwhile, explained that if a boy asks them if they want to receive the images and they say no, the boy will often just send them anyway. She felt that such behaviour is not about intimacy but the boy pursuing their own needs, which she described as "disrespectful" because "they don't really care about your thoughts or feelings" and are "treating you as lesser than them":

Sometimes they'll message and say, 'Do you want me to send it?' And you're like, 'No' and they still do even though it won't benefit you either. It's just a thing for them to do because they want to have done it... they don't use it as a way of flirting or anything like that, I think that they just want to do it.

Some girls recounted being abused by boys if they refuse or do not reciprocate. Magda (14 F), for example, said girls "get violated with different names if you don't say anything to them [the boy]". The girls below attributed such abuse to boys' desire to regain confidence after a refusal:

Ashley (16 F):   Asking for pictures and if you say no, they're like, 'Oh my God, what's wrong with you?'
Emma (16 F):   So, if you said no, they would be like, 'I didn't think you were that great anyway.'

Amelia (16 F): It's almost like an ego or self-confidence thing for them, if you were to say no to doing something then they'll pin that on you instead of like what they did was wrong and then they'll insult you or say something just to give themselves more confidence again.

This gendered landscape of abuse meant that many of the girls were negative about image sharing. One group described it as a "red flag" if a boy wants to share nudes because, they felt, it is indicative of objectification and a lack of respect by the boy toward the girl. When asked whether there are benefits to image sharing, the girls below insisted that any perceived benefits will inevitably be short-lived due to the lack of control they have over the images and the ensuing feelings of shame and guilt for participating in image sharing, as found in other studies (Setty et al., 2022):

Ashley (16 F): I think if they're saying that they have those benefits they're probably kind of short-term and even if they feel empowered sending those things it can still be used against them and along the line, they could regret doing that.

I: **And what is the regret, what happens later down the line?**

Scarlett (16 F): Say if you broke up and at the time you trusted them to have the pictures but then when you break up they still have the pictures and you don't have that same trust with them as you had before but you feel like you can't just message them and say, 'Can you delete them?' cos you can never be certain that they have.

Ashley: I think you also sometimes feel like ashamed because it's an attack on dignity and then the next day I would be like I'm really encouraging this… then you feel guilty…

Their perspectives were related to their perception that boys are praised for image sharing and "proud" (Emma, 16 F), while girls are shamed for violating social conventions and expectations regarding femininity, for example, for girls to be "nice and timid" (Ashley, 16 F). While identifying these issues as problematic, there was a reluctance to report or challenge abusive image sharing both among girls as victim-survivors and young people more broadly as bystanders and witnesses. Several girls spoke instead about ignoring and blocking perpetrators of abuse. Skye (14 F), for example, said she will "block them [perpetrators of unsolicited images and requests for images] straight away and then it's done... [but] it plays in your head for a bit, like the amount of times it has happened", suggesting a residual negative effect of these interactions for her. With boys they know, some girls spoke of couching their refusals in light-hearted terms or through reference to being in the company of a boyfriend, which Lola (16 F) said meant the boy is more likely to be "respectful" toward them. There was a concern among some girls about antagonising boys if they report abuse. For example, Ammy (17 F) described wanting to avoid looking 'uptight':

Ammy: ...if they [the boy] find out you reported it, they have a go at you saying, 'Oh my God, you're too uptight; why would you do this to my mate?'

I: ...you wouldn't want to defend yourself against [that]?

Ammy: Yeah, and then it would go round school and then I would think, maybe I am too uptight.

The anticipated peer reaction constrained the identification and response to abuse and led Ammy to focus on the legitimacy of her reaction to it. Other participants were averse both to reporting to adult authority figures—be they teachers, parents, or police—and to challenging peers who engage in abusive sharing. Regarding adults, participants were concerned, first, about punishment and second, about adults overreacting, mismanaging the situation, and creating further embarrassment for those involved. The young people below, for example, described an imperative among young people to avoid getting themselves or one another into trouble, either for YPSI in general or abusive image sharing specifically:

Usee (13 F):	You don't want your parents and teachers knowing, like getting involved in a situation.
Aye (14 F):	If someone tells, then everyone will turn on that person because they're a snake.
I:	**…what's bad about being a snake?**
Aye:	It depends on the situation. If all your mates get in trouble and everyone is backing each other and there's one person that tells, well, now, everyone is in trouble because that one person has snaked.
Jimmy (14 M):	All the others are lying to just get out of it. That's what it's all about, getting out of trouble innit? Never wanting to get in it.

A desire for peer acceptance and inclusion coupled with normalised 'anti-snitch' cultures meant they wanted to avoid being stigmatised and ostracised for reporting abuse to adults (also see Lloyd, 2019). They were also concerned about safeguarding and referrals; most considered it better for an incident to 'run its course' and victim-survivors just to 'ride out' any embarrassment or shame, whereas adult involvement was perceived to exacerbate the issue. One participant said that image sharing is meant to be 'private' so the last thing they want is for more people, including adults, to find out. Most nevertheless believed abusive image sharing is a problem, just that the only thing worse was the possibility of adults becoming involved. There was, moreover, little evidence they appreciated the efforts made by adults to prevent abusive image sharing, namely how they had been told that all YPSI is wrong and dangerous and that they should abstain.

Most participants were also reluctant to informally challenge abuse within their peer contexts. I heard several refrains about how a "bad friend is better than no friends", which seemed to make it difficult for them to challenge peers. One, for example, said that friends may "turn against you" and another added that "you don't want to not be mates with someone over something that has nothing to do with you", an attitude that inhibited their willingness to intervene to challenge abuse. Moreover, while taking issue with how adults typically emphasise abstinence, many participants nevertheless felt that abusive sharing may be best prevented by not sharing to begin with and that victim-survivors are responsible for anticipating and avoiding abuse. Overall, therefore, these findings suggest that abusive YPSI is shaped by how young people make meaning and think about the 'world'—in this case gendered practices of sexual and intimate self-expression and consumption and distribution of images—which, through acting as what systems theory refers to as mental models, shapes how they behave in terms of their decisions about image sharing and their treatment of images and their peers. Abuse, therefore, is not inevitable but can be addressed through *surfacing* the beliefs that contribute to harm and devising new visions for an ethical online sexual culture.

Improving the Prevention and Response to Abusive Image Sharing

On the face of it, the 2020 UKCCIS guidance offers a framework for a proportionate and holistic approach to YPSI, including regarding preventative education and response to incidents. Yet, to be implemented effectively in terms of educational and criminal justice practice, there is a need for a *surfacing* of beliefs among both adults and young people, and, in turn, an identification of ways that beliefs may fail to address and/ or exacerbate harm. For example, warning young people that sharing images is likely to result in harm (e.g., arising from the abusive act of further non-consensual sharing of the images) and may work to normalise—rather than challenge—the perpetration of abuse, condone and/or promote victim-blaming, and inhibit reporting (e.g., due to self-blame and/or fears regarding self-incrimination and punishment of oneself and/or peers).

At present, adults assume the role of 'expert' when believing that the best way to protect young people from harm is to deter and eradicate YPSI, including through punitive approaches and/or using a 'pedagogy of regret' (Albury, 2017). As Reynolds (2011) recommends, a critical soft systems approach involves a more diverse range of stakeholders (including young people themselves) identifying the problem, developing objectives, and identifying and implementing solutions. First, adults must surface and reflect on the consequences of their beliefs, both anticipated and unanticipated, intended, and unintended. It may be that warnings or a pedagogy of regret (Albury, 2014) are intended to protect young people from harm. Even relatively progressive and social justice-oriented parents with whom I have spoken are so concerned about the, perhaps very real, reputational, and criminal justice risks of YPSI that they warn their children against ever sharing images through shame-based messaging about the potential consequences. This approach, whether by teachers or parents, is problematic, however, because it fails to equip young people with the knowledge they need to identify and respond to abuse. Instead, consensual and non-consensual sharing is conflated, leading young people to blame themselves and others for abuse (see Krieger, 2017; McGlynn & Rackley, 2017) and for matters of privacy, consent, rights, and responsibility to become lost in undifferentiated messaging (Lee et al., 2013).

The surfacing process should also address gender expectations and norms. For example, I was in an elite boys' school for a study about sexual consent conducted in 2022. I observed a lesson that addressed YPSI where pupils were told that storing a sexual image of a minor on their phone was illegal and so they should never do so. The teacher said if a friend sends them a nude image of a girl, they can 'take a cheeky look' but should then delete it because otherwise they risk getting into trouble. This emphasis on detection and punishment avoidance assumes that boys want to look at images of girls and normalises the privacy violation. Some boys I have spoken to about image sharing indeed have said that they would no longer forward an image of a girl to a friend but would instead show it to them to avoid the digital trail and reduce the likelihood of them getting caught (Setty, 2020a; Setty et al., 2022). I have also been told that the Snapchat 'screenshot alert' function—designed to prevent IBSA through alerting the sender if their image has been screenshot—is being circumvented by young people through using a separate device to capture the image.

Unsurfaced beliefs can also constrain the response to incidents. For example, in a study conducted in 2018/2019 (Setty, 2021), a safeguarding lead recounted an incident of YPSI between a similarly aged boy and girl that came to her attention. She asked the girl if it had been consensual and recommended that she consider her answer before responding because if she says no, the safeguarding lead will have to formally escalate it via the safeguarding channels. The girl unsurprisingly said it was consensual. The safeguarding lead seemed to want to avoid a referral due to reputational concerns and considered it 'easier all round' for everyone to move on from the incident with an informal warning not to share images again. While it cannot be established whether this incident was indeed consensual, it demonstrates the possibility for perverse incentives to emerge without holistic and consistent structures in place designed to prevent, identify, and respond effectively to abuse.

These examples demonstrate the ramifications of trying to prevent and respond YPSI without addressing the causes and wider contexts of abuse and harm; for example, the above teacher's concern about reputational damage arising from a formal safeguarding response is embedded within a wider culture of shame and stigma. If adults were to *surface* such beliefs the system stands to benefit, including in terms of ensuring that preventative education engages with the beliefs held by young people that are implicated in abuse and cause harm. In other words, the shame and stigma that creates risks of reputational damage also underpin the perpetration of abuse, for example, that girls who share images lack self-respect and so do not deserve privacy and can be bullied for image sharing. Education thus needs to address gender double standards, fatalism about abuse, and victim-blaming (see resources by School of Sexuality Education et al., 2020).

It is not, however, sufficient to just *tell* young people that their beliefs are wrong but to interrogate the sociocultural contexts at play. This approach would involve *working with* young people to explore *why* particular beliefs are a problem and to discuss alternative visions or 'objectives' for ethical online cultures (Albury, 2017; Dobson, 2019; Setty, 2019). Hence it is important for adults to have surfaced their beliefs about image sharing, including the conflation of abusive and non-abusive sharing and the corresponding emphasis on preventing abuse through deterring primary image sharing. Adults will then be better placed to promote harm reduction (not eradication) (Phippen & Bond, 2023) through addressing abuse rather than emphasising abstinence and *social justice* through addressing the social inequalities, e.g., around gender, that shape abuse (see Setty et al., 2022). It may be possible for the police to be involved in such preventative education (as recommended by the College of Policing [CoP, 2016]). Yet, there should be recognition that the law may not always be able to address the 'grey areas' of consent (e.g., willing agreement to unwanted image sharing due to feelings of expectation and obligation) nor the deeper-rooted sociocultural causes of abuse. Preventative education cannot, therefore, be 'outsourced' the police, which may require schools and police to identify and align their objectives.

It is, moreover, important to conceive of prevention as intimately tied with responding to incidents. Prevention must also entail creating dialogue with young people, so they feel safe and willing to report abuse that they experience or witness. Young people express a desire for safe and non-judgmental avenues for reporting and receiving support where the focus is on the perpetrator and victim-survivors are not blamed or held responsible (Jørgensen et al., 2019; McGeeney & Hanson, 2017; Quayle & Cariola, 2019; Ringrose et al., 2021). As part of surfacing adultist beliefs, therefore, there should be a focus on how potentially well-meaning attempts to deter primary image sharing may be counterproductive in terms of inhibiting reporting. Instead, there needs to be a clear message that victim-survivors should come forward regardless of any image sharing on their part. While educators may want to inform young people about the law on illicit imagery of minors and are mandated to do so by the DfE (2019), they should also inform them about 'Outcome 21' and the fact that consensual sharing among similarly aged minors is unlikely to be met with a criminal justice response. Such messaging entails having shifted objectives from preventing all image sharing to encouraging the reporting of abuse.

It is also important to address the cultural and contextual barriers to reporting. This includes surfacing and challenging so-called anti-snitch cultures but also equipping young people with the skills and emotional literacy they need for positive bystander intervention. This may entail giving specific tools and linguistic options that feel safe to use within these peer contexts. For example, in the lockdown study there was some available vernacular around behaviour being "not cool" or "tight" that participants recounted using to encourage one another to reflect and stop or change their behaviour. It may also entail broadening the conceptualisation of bystander intervention to include the systems of reward and social capital that young people collectively produce and sustain within peer culture (see Albury, 2017; Setty, 2019). Young people can be helped to recognise the role they play and the scope available to them to challenge the facilitating contexts of abuse, for example, by not shaming victim-survivors nor celebrating the actions of perpetrators.

Addressing abusive image sharing in these ways requires the active participation of young people in surfacing beliefs, identifying problems, articulating their objectives and what a 'good' outcome would look like, and developing solutions (see guidance by Setty et al., 2021). Young people should be invited to explore why individuals may perpetrate abuse and what is needed to help victim-survivors, bystanders, and witnesses feel able and willing to challenge and report it, both within peer culture and in terms of the structures of the educational and criminal justice systems that are seeking to prevent and respond to it. It is perhaps unlikely that adult authorities will ever be told about or capable of preventing or responding to every incident. Instead, young people must be given realistic tools that they can use in their peer contexts themselves and this requires working with them to identify the tools and support they need but in ways that surface their underlying beliefs and address those that are implicated in harm.

While important to disentangle abusive from non-abusive image sharing, it is nevertheless advisable not to just shift blame and stigma to 'perpetrators' and instead 'call people in' to a deeper discussion and process of learning about *why* something is harmful and how to create change. Such approaches must be balanced to be 'trauma-informed' and provide due recognition and support for victim-survivors while also recognising that young people who perpetrate abuse should have an opportunity to learn and grow from these experiences.

Conclusion

Presently, schools must educate about abusive image sharing while also telling young people that any form of image sharing is illegal and wrong. This quandary has resulted from an increased emphasis on not unduly criminalising young people and a genuine desire to prevent and respond to abusive image sharing, coupled with the fact that YPSI remains illegal and schools must acknowledge this fact and respond and educate accordingly. The stated intention of the police and CPS not to criminalise consensual image sharing among young people may not, therefore, be being fully communicated to young people, perhaps due to an ongoing desire to promote abstinence from image sharing in entirety.

It is beyond the scope of this chapter to outline the longstanding and well-documented problems with abstinence-based approaches to RSHE and the flaws in the conceptualisations of youth socio-sexual development that underpin these approaches. Yet, as has been explored, this approach to YPSI creates and reinforces barriers to reporting abuse and to holistically and effectively tackling the underlying causes. There is, I would argue, a need to surface ongoing adultist beliefs about image sharing that shape prevention and response practices on the ground and, in turn, change the messaging about YPSI and create safe avenues for reporting and recourse for victim-survivors. It requires surfacing and reflecting on the goal of preventative education and responses to incidents. Is it about stopping all YPSI or about reducing harm as far as possible and seeking social justice for stigmatised groups who are at risk of experiencing abuse? The latter requires a consistent approach to distinguishing non-consensual and abusive image sharing from consensual and developmentally normative digital intimacies and challenging the socio-cultural contexts of inequity and power that shape both the perpetration of abuse and the ensuing shame and blame of victim-survivors.

If such an approach is adopted, we can hope to evidence its effectiveness through observing young people identify and articulate the nature and cause of abuse with nuance and avoid the fatalism and victim-blaming that proliferates. In turn, there may be an improved response to victim-survivors and increased reporting and bystander intervention.

Therefore, any seeming increase in abuse should not be seen as necessarily a bad thing, but expected before hopefully then seeing a fall when the preventative efforts embed themselves. The system will then need to respond to the increase, however, through trauma-informed interventions that involve constructive solutions that delineate the abuse, support victim-survivors, and provide opportunities for perpetrators, and the wider peer collective, to reflect and learn.

Summary

- Sexual and intimate image sharing among young people is a form of digital intimacies that may be consensual and developmentally normative in nature.
- It may, however, involve aggravated or abusive elements, including the non-consensual further sharing of images, unsolicited image sharing, pressure to share images, non-consensual production of images, and coercion to produce images.
- Education and criminal justice policy regarding youth produced sexual imagery (YPSI) have become somewhat nuanced in recent years with increasing recognition of the distinctions between developmentally normative and abusive sharing and an emphasis on not unduly criminalising young people who consensually share images with similarly aged peers.
- Yet, educational interventions and responses to YPSI are often shaped by adultist beliefs about the nature and cause of the problem and do not address the deep-rooted contextual causes of abusive image sharing and may create or exacerbate barriers to reporting by victim-survivors, bystanders, and witnesses of abuse.
- There is a need to instead raise young people's awareness about abusive image sharing and tackle the underlying dynamics of power, reward, stigma, and shame within peer culture that shape the perpetration of and response to abuse. It is also necessary to create safe avenues for reporting and to address the contextual and cultural barriers to reporting and challenging abusive image sharing that exist both within the peer culture and, oftentimes, in the structures of the systems

of prevention and response within education and criminal justice themselves.

- There is a need to surface and address adultist beliefs and shift to an approach that focuses on harm reduction and social justice objectives. Prevention efforts would, in turn, entail surfacing young people's beliefs about the nature and causes of harm and address those that shape and facilitate abuse, including the sociocultural norms and processes at play. The emphasis should be on ensuring that young people feel able and willing to challenge and/or report abuse, and reducing its occurrence through addressing the normative contexts in which it takes place, including as pertain to school and police cultures and practices themselves.
- The approach needs to involve the active participation of young people in surfacing beliefs and then in finding solutions. It must recognise that adults are unlikely to ever be told about or otherwise find out about all incidents of abusive image sharing and instead equip young people with the tools they need to make change themselves in their peer cultures.
- Addressing abusive image sharing likely requires deemphasising the deterrence of all YPSI in general in favour of improving the prevention, reporting, and response to abuse.

References

Albury, K. (2014). Porn and sex education, porn as sex education. *Porn Studies, 1*(1–2), 172–181.

Albury, K. (2017). Just because it's public doesn't mean it's any of your business: Adults' and children's sexual rights in digitally mediated spaces. *New Media and Society, 19*(5), 713–725.

Arthur, R. (2018). Consensual teenage sexting and youth criminal records. *Criminal Law Review, 5*, 377–383.

Bond, E., & Phippen, A. (2019). *Police response to youth offending around the generation and distribution of indecent images of children and its implications.*

University of Suffolk. https://www.uos.ac.uk/sites/default/files/FOI-Report-Final-Outcome-21.pdf

Checkland, P., & Poulter, J. (2020). Soft systems methodology. In M. Reynolds & S. Howell (Eds.), *Systems approaches to making change: A practical guide* (pp. 201–253). Springer.

Churchman, C. W. (1968). *The systems approach.* Dell Publishing Company.

College of Policing (CoP). (2016). *Briefing note: Police action in response to youth produced sexual imagery ('sexting').* CoP. https://library.college.police.uk/docs/college-of-policing/briefing-note-sexting-2016.pdf

Cooper, K., Quayle, E., Jonsson, L., & Svedin, C. G. (2016). Adolescents and self-taken sexual images: A review of the literature. *Computers in Human Behavior, 55,* 706–716.

Crown Prosecution Service (CPS). (2018). *Social media: Guidelines for prosecuting cases involving communications on social media.* CPS. https://www.cps.gov.uk/legal-guidance/social-media-guidelines-prosecuting-cases-involving-communications-sent-social-media

Department for Education (DfE). (2019). *Statutory guidance on RSE for schools in England.* DfE. https://www.gov.uk/government/publications/relationships-education-relationships-and-sex-education-rse-and-health-education

Department for Education (DfE). (2021). *Sexual violence and sexual harassment between children in schools and colleges.* DfE. https://assets.publishing.service.gov.uk/government/uploads/system/uploads/attachment_data/file/1014224/Sexual_violence_and_sexual_harassment_between_children_in_schools_and_colleges.pdf

Department for Education (DfE). (2022). *Keping children safe in education.* DfE. https://www.gov.uk/government/publications/keeping-children-safe-in-education--2

Dobson, A. S. (2019). 'The things you didn't do': Gender, slut-sham-ing, and the need to address sexual harassment in narrative resources responding to sexting and cyberbullying. In H. Vandebosch & L. Green (Eds.), *Narratives in research and interventions on cyberbullying among young people* (pp. 147–160). Springer.

Doyle, C., Douglas, E., & O'Reilly, G. (2021). The outcomes of sexting for children and adolescents: A systematic review of the literature. *Journal of Adolescence, 92*(1), 86–113. https://doi.org/10.1016/j.adolescence.2021.08.009

García-Gómez, A. (2017). Teen girls and sexual agency: Exploring the intrapersonal and intergroup dimensions of sexting. *Media, Culture and Society, 39*(3), 391–407.

Guice, J. (2015). Keeping faith with Ferber: why states may criminalise sexual imaging of minors above the age of consent for sexual activity. *Social Science Research Network.* http://papers.ssrn.com/sol3/papers.cfm?abstract_id=2559869

Hales, H. (2018). *A 'sexting surge' or a conceptual muddle?* Police Foundation. https://www.police-foundation.org.uk/2018/01/sexting-surge-conceptual-muddle/

Henry, N., Flynn, A., & Powell, A. (2018). Policing image-based sexual abuse: Stakeholder perspectives. *Police Practice and Research, 19*(6), 565–581.

Jørgensen, C. R., Weckesser, A., Turner, J., & Wade, A. (2019). Young people's views on sexting education and support needs: Findings and recommendations from a UK-based study. *Sex Education, 19*(1), 25–40.

Krieger, M. A. (2017). Unpacking 'sexting': A systematic review of nonconsensual sexting in legal, educational, and psychological literatures. *Trauma, Violence, and Abuse, 18*(5), 593–601.

Leary, M. G. (2008). Self-produced child pornography: The appropriate societal response to juvenile self-sexual exploitation. *Virginia Journal of Social Policy and the Law, 15*(1), 1–50.

Lee, M., Crofts, T., McGovern, A., & Milivojevici, S. (2015). *Sexting and young people.* Basingstoke.

Lee, M., Crofts, T., Salter, M., Milivojevic, S., & McGovern, A. (2013). 'Let's get sexting': Risk, power, sex and criminalisation in the moral domain. *International Journal for Crime, Justice and Social Democracy, 2*(1), 35–49.

Lloyd, J. (2019). Response and interventions into harmful sexual behaviour in schools. *Child Abuse and Neglect, 94*, 104037.

McGeeney, E., & Hanson, E. (2017). *Digital Romance: A research project exploring young people's use of technology in their romantic relationships and love lives.* National Crime Agency and Brook. https://www.basw.co.uk/system/files/resources/basw_85054-7.pdf

McGlynn, C., & Rackley, E. (2017). Image-based sexual abuse. *Oxford Journal of Legal Studies, 37*(3), 534–561.

Moran-Ellis, J. (2012). Sexting, intimacy and criminal acts: Translating teenage sexualities. In P. Johnson & D. Dalton (Eds.), *Policing sex* (pp. 115–132). Routledge.

National Police Chiefs' Council. (2016a). *A common sense police approach to investigating sexting among under-18s.* https://news.npcc.police.uk/releases/a-common-sense-police-approach-to-investigating-sexting-among-under-18s

National Police Chiefs' Council. (2016b). *Guidance for disclosure.* https:// assets.publishing.service.gov.uk/government/uploads/system/uploads/attach ment_data/file/578979/GD8_-_Sexting_Guidance.pdf

Ofsted. (2021). *Review of sexual abuse in schools and colleges.* Department for Education. https://www.gov.uk/government/publications/review-of-sex ual-abuse-in-schools-and-colleges/review-of-sexual-abuse-in-schools-and-col leges

Phippen, A., & Bond, E. (2023). *Policing teen sexting: Supporting children's rights while applying the law.* Springer International Publishing Cham.

Phippen, A., & Street, L. (2022). *Online resilience and wellbeing in young people.* Palgrave Macmillan.

Quayle, E., & Cariola, L. (2019). Management of non-consensually shared youth-produced sexual images: A Delphi study with adolescents as experts. *Child Abuse and Neglect, 95*, 104064.

Ravn, S., Coffey, J., & Roberts, S. (2021). The currency of images: Risk, value and gendered power dynamics in young men's accounts of sexting. *Feminist Media Studies, 21*(2), 315–331.

Reynolds, M. (2011). Critical thinking and systems thinking: Towards a critical literacy for systems thinking in practice. In C. P. Horvath & J. M. Forte (Eds.), *Critical thinking* (pp. 37–68). Nova Science Publishers.

Ringrose, J., Gill, R., Livingstone, S., & Harvey, L. (2012). *A qualitative study of children, young people and 'sexting': A report prepared for the NSPCC.* https://eprints.lse.ac.uk/44216/1/__Libfile_repository_Content_Livings tone%2C%20S_A%20qualitative%20study%20of%20children%2C%20y oung%20people%20and%20%27sexting%27%20%28LSE%20RO%29. pdf

Ringrose, J., & Harvey, L. (2015). Boobs, back-off, six packs and bits: Medi-ated body parts, gendered reward, and sexual shame in teens' sexting images. *Continuum Journal of Media and Cultural Studies, 29*(2), 205–217.

Ringrose, J., Whitehead, S., & Regehr, K. (2021). 'Wanna trade?': Cisheteronormative homosocial masculinity and the normalization of abuse in youth digital sexual image exchange. *Journal of Gender Studies, 31*(2), 243–261.

School of Sexuality Education, Ringrose, J., Mendes, K., & Horeck, T. (2020). *Online sexual harassment. Comprehensive guidance for schools.* School of Sexuality Education. https://static1.squarespace.com/static/57dbe276f7e0 abec416bc9bb/t/5f86b37c409ee95b26cf27e6/1602663308003/School+of+ Sex+Ed+OSH+Comprehensive+Guidance.pdf

Scott, R. H., Smith, C., Formby, E., Hadley, A., Hallgarten, L., Hoyle, A., Marston, C., McKee, A., & Tourountsis, D. (2020). What and how: Doing good research with young people, digital intimacies, and relationships and sex education. *Sex Education, 20*(6), 675–691.

Setty, E. (2019). A rights-based approach to youth sexting: Challenging risk, shame, and the denial of rights to bodily and sexual expression within youth digital sexual culture. *International Journal of Bullying Prevention, 1*(4), 298–311.

Setty, E. (2020a). *Risk and harm in youth sexting culture: Young people's perspectives.* Routledge.

Setty, E. (2020b). 'Confident' and 'hot' or 'desperate' and 'cowardly'? Meanings of young men's sexting practices in youth sexting culture. *Journal of Youth Studies, 23*(5), 561–577.

Setty, E. (2021). Sex and consent in contemporary youth sexual culture: The 'ideals' and the 'realities.' *Sex Education, 21*(3), 331–346.

Setty, E., & Dobson, E. (2022). Department for Education statutory guidance for Relationships and Sex Education in England: A rights-based approach? *Archives of Sexual Behavior.* https://doi.org/10.1007/s10508-022-02340-5

Setty, E., Ringrose, J., & Regehr, K. (2022). Digital sexual violence and the gendered constraints of consent in youth image sharing. In M. Horvarth & J. Brown (Eds.), *Rape: A challenge to contemporary thinking—10 years on* (2nd ed., pp. 45–61). Routledge.

Setty, E., School of Sexuality Education, & Fumble. (2021). *Transforming school cultures through Relationships and Sex Education.* University of Surrey. https://transformingschoolculture.wordpress.com/guidance-for-schools-on-designing-and-delivering-safe-and-effective-rse/

Sexual Offences Act (2003). HMSO.

Thomas, S. E. (2018). 'What should I do?': Young women's reported dilemmas with nude photographs. *Sexuality Research and Social Policy, 15*(2), 192–207.

UK Council for Internet Safety. (2020). *Sharing nudes and semi-nudes: Advice for education settings working with children and young people.* DCMS and UK Council for Internet Safety. https://www.gov.uk/government/publications/sharing-nudes-and-semi-nudes-advice-for-education-settings-working-with-children-and-young-people

Wolak, J., Finkelhor, D., Walsh, W., & Treitman, L. (2018). Sextortion of minors: Characteristics and dynamics. *Journal of Adolescent Health, 62*(1), 72–79.

Systemic Responses to Online Abuse on Campus

Katie Tyrrell, Andy Phippen, and Emma Bond

Introduction

Systems theory approaches are rarely applied in online safeguarding contexts. Not helped, we would suggest, due to the single stakeholder focus on a lot of the policy discussions around online safeguarding in the UK (UK Government, 2022) and EU (European Union, 2019), which suggest online safeguarding is solely the domain of platform and service providers. Although Firmin (2020) argues whole systems and contextual approaches to resolve peer-on-peer abuse in school setting, this does not specifically consider online safeguarding. However, elements of systems

K. Tyrrell · E. Bond
University of Suffolk, IPSWICH, UK
e-mail: k.tyrrell@uos.ac.uk

E. Bond
e-mail: e.bond@uos.ac.uk

A. Phippen (✉)
Bournemouth University, Bournemouth, UK
e-mail: aphippen1@bournemouth.ac.uk

© The Author(s), under exclusive license to Springer Nature
Switzerland AG 2024
O. Adisa and E. Bond (eds.), *Tackling Domestic Abuse and Sexual Violence*, Palgrave
Studies in Victims and Victimology, https://doi.org/10.1007/978-3-031-58600-2_8

theory, such as the importance of feedback between elements and the influence of interconnected components (Berlinski, 1970), we would argue, are exactly the knowledge required to break online safeguarding approaches out of their simplistic, single duty of care, perspective.

However, we argue that there is a well-established systems approach that is applicable to this context, namely Bronfenbrenner's (1979) Ecology of Child Development. Bronfenbrenner's seminal work applied both nature and nurture perspectives to a child's development stating that their own biology is central to their development, but interactions with other actors in their environment, such as family, community, and society all play a part in development and an action in one of these actors will impact across the wider ecosystem of development. While there have been criticisms of Bronfenbrenner's approach and the application of his approach (e.g., see Tudge et al., 2016), particular around complexity, cultural variation, and specificity, it is a well-established model that embraces the systems theory approach effectively and has been readily applied to social care contexts (e.g., Pardeck, 1988).

Therefore, we can conclude, in order to provide the most effective context for child development, we should not just look at the child, but its environment as well. While one could argue that the concept of Adverse Childhood Experiences (Hardt & Rutter, 2004), which underpins the popular Trauma Informed Schools approach (Wiest-Stevenson & Lee, 2016) used in a lot of UK schools adopts a form of systems thinking, it, again, lacks any focus around online abuse and subsequent harms. We have developed the Bronfenbrenner model to consider the ecosystem around online safeguarding and highlighted its applicability to both child (Phippen & Bond, 2020a) and adult online safeguarding (Bond & Phippen, 2022a).

In this chapter, we argue that the same approach can be beneficial in Higher Education settings, providing empirical evidence to show that the current UK university environment is failing to embrace this environmental approach and, at best, adopts an ad hoc approach where system dependencies are not well understood (particularly from the perspective of the student) and at worst, completely lacking. We argue that attempts to 'encourage' the sector to take online safeguarding seriously have failed, and there is a need for the formal regulation more familiar in the statutory sector as a means for the exosystem to impose great influence on the system as a whole. In developing this analysis, we propose a development of the Bronfenbrenner model that is applicable to the Higher Education setting. While the concept of the whole can be challenging when applied to complex systems (Nicolis & Prigogine, 1989) such as a university, particularly when considering the human actors with the system, the model is a useful tool to articulate the interconnection between the elements within a university system with a duty of care to its students and the role of multiple stakeholders in delivering this.

Online Safeguarding in Higher Education

Online safeguarding—the policies and practices in institutions to ensure that people to whom they have a duty of care are protected from harm, abuse, or exploitation while using the online or digital technologies—has traditionally been focussed upon organisations who have a statutory duties, such as school and colleges. However, there is a growing concern that the role of online abuse in domestic abuse and harassment needs to be better understood among adult populations (Afrouz, 2023; Leitão, 2021; Robbins et al., 2016). Organisations who have a duty of care toward staff and other stakeholders should also consider how online abuse is tackled and how victims of abuse can be subsequently supported. This is as applicable to universities as to other organisations with adult stakeholders.

The nature of online harms toward adults is only recently being considered as a serious issue. As Davidson et al. (2019, p. 1) suggest:

> The development of email and social media platforms has changed the way in which people interact with each other. The open sharing of personal data in public forums has resulted in online harassment in its many forms becoming increasingly problematic. The number of people having negative online experiences is increasing, with close to half of adult internet users reporting having seen hateful content online in the past year.

While some literature attempts to define specific acts, such as those that are acting by someone on the person (e.g., cyberstalking or online harassment) or those that make use of technology to facilitate the abuse (Brown et al., 2018; Messing et al., 2020, p. 10), definitions remain contested. As such, online harassment remains a broad term, which includes many negative experiences online, (e.g., offensive name calling, purposeful embarrassment, physical threats, sustained harassment, stalking, and sexual harassment) and thus, due to the lack of definition, online harassment is considered to vary by person and by context (Davidson et al., 2019).

Nevertheless, Brook (2019) revealed that, while 56% of students have been subject to unwanted sexual experiences, only 15% realised they have been sexually harassed. Moreover, a quarter of women (26%) had been sent unwanted sexually explicit messages but only 3% reported it. The research also showed that some groups of students are more vulnerable to online harassment, for example, due to disability, ethnicity, sexuality, or religious belief. However, due to their protected characteristics, they are even more unlikely to come forward to disclose abuse.

Online harms are well acknowledged in the compulsory educational sector, with statutory instruments (Department for Education, 2022) and regulation (Ofsted, 2022) providing the appropriate frameworks to make institutions aware of their responsibilities and how they might address online safeguarding in their settings. However, as discussed above, online harms do not cease when young people enter into late adolescence and early adulthood, and yet we see little evidence of similar regulatory controls being introduced in the Higher Education sector.

While the sector has made attempts to make institutions and senior leaders aware of the potential for harm online, and the need for student-centric and supportive responses, there is still a perception it would be better if institutions did this without regulatory demand. The launch of the Universities UK (UUK)—the membership body for Higher Education Institutions in the UK—'Changing the Culture' report in 2016 exposed the experiences of violence against women, hate crime, and harassment affecting university students and called for further action to specifically tackle online harassment and hate crime. However, little response from the sector in spite of expectations of a duty of care accorded to universities in the UK to act reasonably in students' best interests, to protect their well-being, and provide appropriate support, resulted in further 'encouragement' from UUK who launched their Tackling Online Harms and Promoting Online Welfare report in September 2019 (Universities UK, 2022). With growing pressure from media (e.g., BBC News, 2018a, 2018b, 2019) the Office for Students (2021), the regulatory body for universities in the UK published a Statement of Expectations on Harassment and Sexual Misconduct.

This statement called on universities to tackle issues related to harassment and sexual misconduct and stated, '*Our definitions include harassment and sexual misconduct through any medium, including, for example, online.*' However, it was disappointing that this statement did not differentiate online harms from other forms of abuse. It stated a number of expectations which adopted best practice approaches around safeguarding, incorporating whole institution approaches, student voice, effective policy and practice, training, and transparency of disclosure and investigation. However, its impact and value to student victims of online abuse remains contested, and there are challenges to the voluntary nature of the expectation (Sums Consulting, 2022). Ahmed (2021) explored at length the response of universities to harassment disclosures in general and found the sector lacking in its duty of care, with institutions more concerned with their reputation and management of external communications rather than support for victims. Indeed, in Ahmed's findings there was significant evidence of institutions applying power and control over victims with the implementation of restitution only after binding in a non-disclosure agreement. We present further evidence below that institutions in general are not equipped to support victims and, in some cases, argue that is it simply not their concern.

We know in the statutory education sector that there was a massive shift in the development of policy and practice around online safeguarding after it was announced the Ofsted would inspect specifically around these issues (Phippen, 2016). However, within the HE sector, while there is now guidance, we would argue that policy and practice in the sector is still ad hoc, and there is very little appropriate guidance.

The State of the Sector

As we have detailed above, there has been much discussion about changing the culture in Higher Education around student safeguarding and how difficult this is. However, we would argue that the focus on cultural challenge and strategic levers fails to acknowledge the student/victim-survivors in these discussions and such top-level debates fail to instil the urgency of need in supporting real people whose lives can be significantly impacted as the result of online abuse. While institutional buy in is crucial, it only considers the role of a single stakeholder in the safeguarding of students—the institution itself, which conflicts with systems approaches that highlight the importance of engagement across diverse stakeholders in the system (Stroh, 2015). In developing our arguments further, we draw upon two sources of empirical data, authentic student voice and institutional response to Freedom of Information requests, which highlight how the sector is, currently, letting down victims of abuse.

Student Voice

In this analysis authentic student voice was analysed through discussions with 20 students who engaged in 5 focus groups. These focus groups were conducted in 2019, using in person discussions, and the focus of the discussions was the role of technology in intimate relationships. Students were aged between 18 and 25, with an average age of 21. Groups were mixed sex, with 10 females and 10 males participating in the discussions.

Data was collected via semi-structured focus group interviews, lasting between 60 and 90 minutes with students at a university. After the announcement of the COVID-19 lockdown, students who were still based at the university or continued their studies at the university were contacted to see if they would be happy to engage in a follow-up interview. Five of the above students, who were still at the university, were followed up in 2020 during the COVID-19 pandemic to identify any potential influence of COVID-19 upon perceptions and experiences of technology use within intimate partner relationships.

While the breadth of discussion and the richness of data is diffi-cult to present in a short book chapter, we can draw and illustrate a number of key issues emerging from these discussions, such as the preva-lence of the issue, the mundanity of attitude toward what can be serious abuse, a passivity in response to the abuse, because victims do not believe anything can be done, and an institutional abdication of responsibility. What comes strongly from this analysis is that without clear guidance and delineation of responsibility, victims of potentially serious abuse can be left feeling that they cannot turn to their institution for support.

While the focus on this chapter lies in the use of digital technology in abuse among student populations and organisational response, we feel it is important to point out that their experiences with digital tech-nology in relationships are generally positive. There were many examples of students seeing the value in digital technology in relationships in a number of ways:

> I think in terms of maintaining relationships... I think the use of What-sApp and stuff is kind of like, it's less kind of stress and strain of having to see them every day or like... we can still talk to each other, so when I have been with people before they kind of want to see me every day and it's like...
>
> whether you're just thinking of purely emotional attachment or a sexual one, that's between you and the person you are messaging... that defeats the ideas of politics, location and rurality, deprivation, because as long as you have got an internet connection, you can share who you are with everyone.

There were certainly many examples of positive use of technology. However, unsurprisingly there were many discussions around the possible harms that result from engaging in relations online, such as ghosting and concerns around authenticity:

> I did match with a guy that goes here and he ghosted me... we never met up, he was a student paramedic, like oh do you want to go out for coffee, and he was like yeah sounds good and then he just didn't reply.
>
> Usually when talking about relationships online and meeting people online the first thing that comes to mind is are they the person they

really claim to be, you know, Tinder and all this stuff it's really hard to know the person that is behind the screen... it broadens your chances but at the same time it is dangerous.

However, there were a number of narratives that introduced the concept of power and control in relationships and the role of technology in this. Certainly, technology provides users with a level of information that was never possible in a pre-internet age. For example, information on a partner's location and whether they are online is now, technically, very easy. And because conversations and interactions have a digital trail, there is also the opportunity to explore discourse with others in a manner that would be impossible in pre-internet relationships. However, what seems clear from a lot of the discussion is there is very little recognition of how controlling or unhealthy this is. And in some cases, justifications were made for abuse because of a partner's previous relationships. In that way, the technology provides the means for oddly justified surveillance as reassurance.

> I think the fact that he is able to access my phone sort of helps him deal with that but also makes it worse because he can just go onto my phone and check I have given him my password, and he can go on my phone and check to say oh ok he has a message from this person
> I think she was jealous. I think she, she wanted to know. Or I think, actually, what it was, I think I might have signed into her device with my phone or like through the communal. So, we had like an iPad and stuff. And we both use the iPad. And I just signed in my Facebook and I kind of just left it there. And so, you know, it was kind of transparent.

And while looking at phones to 'reassure' is one element of control in relationships, the discussions also explored excessive communication and tracking, failing to recognise this as harassment.

> ...he would be texting and calling he would be tracking. That's another thing actually, I remember telling him I was getting a taxi, but it was really warm. And we weren't that drunk. So, we just walked home, and he watched me on tracker walk home, waited till I got back to my flat rang me up and bollocked me for not getting a taxi.

… he'd always ring me I'd go to like house parties or flat parties in other flats. And he'd be ringing me, texting me kind of almost guilt tripping me to come home kind of thing.

And some others tried to look at tracking technology as a good thing because, again, it provided reassurance:

Me and [name] don't track each other on Snapmaps, but we have the find my friends on and usually we will keep it off, but because I'm here and he is like 2 hours away, if I've gone out I'll normally put mine on and he can just click notify me when she leaves, so if I'm out, otherwise I do find myself like, where is he, he is down the pub again, erm right….

With my boyfriend we have only been going out for a month so we're not that far into the relationship but his ex was very shady about her phone so whenever she was with him she would always have do not disturb on so she wouldn't get any messages pop up and she wouldn't let him on her phone… but with me I'm like you can have your finger-print on my phone you can go on it whenever you want I've got nothing to hide

A further factor that makes digital technology particularly problematic in relationship is the means to always be in touch and the repercussions if that does not happen. There was a view, by some students that you had to be available and should always be responsive:

If I didn't respond for hours, I'd be dead

… with Facebook it tells you when you're last active, you say goodnight to someone, and you stay on your phone because you're a human being and you just go on random stuff and they're like you're still active, who are you talking too, uhoh… I'm just on Twitter!

What is particularly concerning, but not unexpected, with some of the discussions was the normalisation of these behaviours which would have been viewed as extremely unusual and also perhaps more easily recognised as abuse in the offline world:

> There was a girl on my course and her boyfriend cheated on her so she has installed a tracker on his phone, so at any given time she can see exactly where he is..., she looks through his phone all the time, she tells us

In exploring the role of their institution in providing support should the issues in relationships cause concern and upset, we could see lots of evidence that students were extremely unclear regarding whether they should expect support.

> That's the issue, if it happens at the university on campus then it's the universities problem, if it doesn't then it's not, they have to condemn it, they have to say I don't know without any far stretch of the imagination, anything to do with PR, but from what either way, the way I see it you have to condemn it ...
>
> that's not necessarily their responsibility to enforce it but they need to let people know if you do this stuff there will be people who will enforce it ...but as a university they need to let people know that people are doing it, and that these are the people who have the authority to do it...
>
> I think the only case in which a university could have an issue is if it occurred in a building perhaps there is remit there... I think the only thing the university could provide is counselling related to online disputes or online relationships

What is clear from these discussions is that students make a great deal of use of technology in their personal relationships and, in a lot of cases, it is a positive thing. However, as we have shown above there were also plenty of example of students being victims of abuse and coercive control and, in some cases, not recognising it as such. Furthermore, they are not sure even if a university should be providing support, even though these relationships arise because of being placed in environments because of being at university, with other members of the university community. Again, this highlights the importance of the need for clarity around the roles of the institution and their role within a broader system of stakeholders, as well as the multiple roles the institution might play. For example, while they should be providing routes for disclosure and policies to articulate response, there should also be playing a role in developing knowledge and awareness so victims recognise abuse and how to get support.

However, this does pose the question—are universities equipped to provide this support?

Institutional Responses

In further research (Bond & Phippen, 2022b) we adopted an approach to survey all institutions using Freedom of Information legislation. The Freedom of Information Act 2000 (UK Government, 2000) in England, Wales and Northern Ireland, and the Freedom of Information Act (Scotland, 2002; UK Government, 2002) allow us to request information from public bodies (and UK universities are public bodies) and expect a response within a reasonable time period (normally 20 working days). Within these requests we wished to explore the different elements of what we would view as best practice around safeguarding.

Namely:

- Policy.
- Senior management accountability.
- Training and awareness.
- Routes for disclosure.
- Clarity of investigation approaches.
- Data collection and recording.

Upon issuing the request, we had one request to clarify what we meant by student safeguarding because it seemed they did not believe that, as a university, had any safeguarding duties due to the lack of minors in their care:

> We have been asked to clarify your definition of "student safeguarding" as the University would normally use the term "safeguarding" concerns raised about individuals under the age of 18.

Which we feel highlights the important of statutory instruments to ensure universities recognise their responsibility and do not so easily shirk them. In total we received responses from 130 HEIs.

Across the 130 HEIs who responded to our request, there were a total of 21 types of different policies in the student body which were identified as addressing how the institution tackles online abuse (including image-based abuse and online harassment) or hate speech online. In total, we were sent 266 policies from our 130 responding institutions. We received at least one policy from 121 HEIs, suggesting that the other eight did not believe they had policy to cover this. However, we developed a keyword analysis algorithm so we could search the 266 policies to ensure the claims made by the institutions were matched in the reality of their policies.

Almost 60% of the policies provided by institutions where they claimed coverage of online harassment and abuse had no mention of 'online' whatsoever. While 'harassment' was well covered, if we consider 'online harassment' as a distinct abusive behaviour, it was hardly covered at all, nor is hate speech or hate crime. While 'social media' did receive coverage in just over 50% of policies, a lot of those policies related to social media conduct (i.e., 'think before you post') rather than the use of these platforms to abuse or harass.

We also asked for the name person in charge of safeguarding for the university. 110 of the 130 HEIs who replied had a named person responsible, but 15 did not and five refused to respond to the question. We did, however, have a few responses as that illustrated below:

> The university is not obligated to hold these designated roles. As we are a Higher Education Institution, this places us in a different position to school/college institutions and we are not required to designate specific person(s) to be directly responsible for safeguarding.

Once again highlighted the importance of regulation to 'encourage' good practice.

We also asked if there was a board member who was responsible for safeguarding. This is important because board scrutiny is often another good driver of good practice. Only 43 respondents had a named member of their university governing body/board directly responsible for student safeguarding.

We also asked HEIs to provide details of how students can report incidents of online abuse (including image-based abuse and online harassment) or hate speech online in their institution. Like the findings in relation to the policies, we found a wide variety of responses, including the student complaints process; pastoral support systems, student services, student welfare officers, and a range of reporting mechanisms. While there was certainly a great deal of variety to manage disclosures, what there was not, was consistency.

We also asked about the training of staff. The information provided allowed us to probe more deeply into sectoral knowledge around online harassment, abuse, and hate speech and also attempted to gain a deeper understanding of why recording incident levels of online abuse in the sector seems so low. Alongside policy, training is an essential part of the foundation for effective support of students who might be affected by online harassment. Without effective training and policy, we cannot hold any confidence that an institution is capable of supporting students who become victims of online abuse when they have neither a documented response nor knowledgeable staff to support them.

54% of respondents claimed some level of staff training around online abuse. This means almost half of the institutions in the sector provide no training. Of those who do provide training, the vast majority (96%) said that online abuse, harassment, and hate speech are tackled within 'generic' training—this reflects the Office for Student's view the online abuse is simply part of other forms of abuse. We had one respondent reply to say there was no need for training on online abuse because it was the same as the offline equivalent.

Finally, we asked whether universities worked with external bodies, to whom they could learn or refer student victims. We were unsurprised to discover that the vast majority (73%) of respondents stated that they had no links to external agencies. Again, in considering a whole systems approach to tackling abuse in this context, the failure to acknowledge the role of external bodies is concerning.

Of those who did (27%), there were a variety of links reported, such as police, sexual assault referral units, domestic violence NGOs, mental health support, Rape Crisis, the Revenge Porn helpline, and Victim Support. Interestingly, the majority of those reported had little specialism around online abuse.

Clearly, we would like to see the university sector take their duty of care responsibilities seriously related to supporting students who are the victims of online abuse, and we would rather the sector responded because they believe student welfare, effective reporting, and consistent staff training are all good things to do, rather than things they will resist until statutory duties are imposed. Such discrepancies across the sector mean that a student who is a victim of online abuse, harassment, or hate speech is treated by their university not just down to where they are, but also to whom they are speaking.

A Failing Sector

Drawing together empirical data from both of these investigations, we can conclude that:

1. Students are frequently exposed to online harms and sometimes do not recognise them as such.
2. Students are not clear that their university has a duty of care around their well-being.
3. Universities have, in general, quite an ad hoc approach to online harms and at best will incorporate it into more general abuse policies.
4. Universities do not know how to respond to disclosures around online harms because their staff are not sufficiently trained and there is not sufficient senior leadership scrutiny to make this happen.
5. Many universities are trying to do something, but that something is inconsistent. This is unsurprising given the lack of consistency of expectation from the regulator.

These data sets also motivated us to develop our thinking around what best practice might look like. Our conclusions were twofold:

1. Universities do not tackle online harms effectively because they do not recognise the roles of different stakeholders (or systems) in student safeguarding
2. Universities do not know what a systems approach looks like

While there are, arguably, increasing policy drivers for systems change within the Higher Education sector, for example, a statement of expectations from the UK universities regulator, we argue that this will change little for student bodies without wholesale institutional system change. Such university-wide change requires consideration of context and required input at all system levels, from senior management responsibilities and support to policy, training, and appropriate routes for disclosure. We know from our data that universities are getting it very wrong. They are reactive and working in isolation, rather than adopting whole system approaches.

In terms of understanding the role of different stakeholders (incorporating a whole systems approach) we have, in recent years, defined a stakeholder model for online safeguarding, which is an adaptation of the seminal work of Bronfenbrenner (1979) and his ecological framework of child development. It is as applicable in this context as others.

Perhaps the most important of Bronfenbrenner's model was the importance of mesosystems—the interactions between the different players in subject's development. Arguably, this is something we have lost sight of in the broad online safeguarding world, including that which considers the support of adults. By adapting this ecosystem for online safety, we can see both the breadth of stakeholder responsibilities for safeguarding and how the stakeholders interact (Fig. 1).

- Personal—Peers, friends, family
- Institution—training, student services, tutors, administrators, awareness raising,
- Community—safeguarding organisations and support services
- Influences—Mass media, industry, legal system, policy, national agencies, social movements (e.g., MeToo, BLM)
- Ideologies—Rights frameworks, democratic institutions

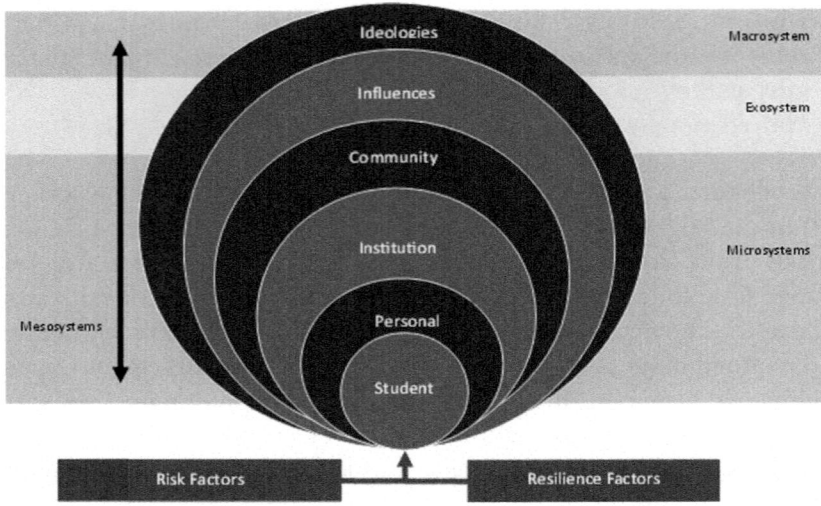

Fig. 1 The student online safety ecosystem

The value of the model is that it shows the many different stake-holders in online safeguarding and shows the importance of interactions (mesosystems) between them, as well as the distance a given stakeholder is from the student we wish to safeguard. Adopting a more holistic view of working with others to support students in their online risk-taking and decision-making is far more effective, as stakeholders can bring their own expertise to the safeguarding role.

There are many microsystems around the student, with whom the student directly interacts with before we even approach the place of technology providers in this safeguarding model. From the broad policy perspective, the focus of solution provision, and also social responsi-bility, it would seem, is entirely within the exosystem. And while we drive our expectations of responsibility at this layer, we lose focus on the roles in the microsystem or the fact that encompassing all of this— the macrosystem—should be the rights of the student. For students, we also need to be mindful that they already bring risk and resilience factors to their student life, and these might be influenced by good and bad educational experiences and good and bad life experiences. It is important to recognise in university safeguarding that the knowledge of students entering the institutional system is not consistent. However, the microsystems still interact and it is important that institutions are mindful of the broad stakeholder space, rather than feeling they need to provide all of the solutions themselves.

In developing the theoretical model for online safeguarding in Higher Education, we have developed a self-review tool for institutions (Bond & Phippen, 2022b). Encapsulating a whole systems approach, informed by the stakeholder model, the tool allows institutions to consider their online safeguarding policy and practice in 25 different aspects, grouped around:

- Policy: The guiding principles related to an aspect of safeguarding that provide the foundation for practice in the institution.
- Education and Training: How and where knowledge and understanding of the issues of online safeguarding is developed in the institution for both staff and students.
- Technology: How technological tools are used to help deliver policy and practice related to online safeguarding.
- Practice: How policy is implemented across the institution to deliver an institutional culture around online safeguarding.

For each of the aspects, the institution can level themselves between level 0 and level 3:

- Level 0—Reactive: There is no policy/practice in place, and issues are dealt with only in a reactive manner
- Level 1—Basic: There is a simply definition of policy or fundamental aspects of practice, but they are not detailed in scope or scale or embedded in routine practice.
- Level 2—Embedded: Policy and practice are embedded and students included in their development. Policies are detailed and proactive, practice is applied across the institution in all departments and faculties.
- Level 3—Holistic: There is a sound understanding of how policy and practice work together to safeguard students online. There is ongoing

reflection of best practice and knowledge sharing across the HEI and with statutory and non-statutory organisations in the community.

A focus on stakeholders, both internal and external, is reiterated within the tool. However, the main goal of the tool is to make institutions aware that online safeguarding is something they need to engage with and it is not something that one or two staff members can tackle in isolation. It is important that university stakeholders, from senior leaders to those with specific student-facing roles all recognise the potential harms and how the institution provides routes for disclosure and transparency of response. Certainly, feedback from those in the sector who have used it shows both the value the guidance and that is also useful to convince senior managers that a pre-emptive whole systems approach is more effective than reactive responses when serious disclosures occur. It is better to acknowledge these issues can occur among the student population, rather than ignoring it until an incident occurs.

However, we have been told that sometimes senior management is less keen in being responsive for one simple reason—they do not have to do it, so they will not, which highlights, once again, the importance of having a strong regulator in the exosystem to provide standards of expectation, rather than hoping institutions will do the right thing. What is clear is the current approach is not working—universities do not know (and in some cases do not care) what to do, and students are unclear about the role of the university in their safeguarding. We propose that a systems approach will more effectively support both universities and students, but we still need policymakers to accept their role in the system as well, rather than hoping universities will do something on their own.

References

Afrouz, R. (2023). The nature, patterns and consequences of technology-facilitated domestic abuse: A scoping review. *Trauma, Violence, & Abuse, 24*(2), 913–927.

Ahmed, S. (2021). *Complaint!*. Duke University Press.

BBC News (2018a). *Exeter University student explains racist message revelation.* https://www.bbc.co.uk/news/newsbeat-43987148. Accessed November 2022.

BBC News (2018b). *Plymouth University Tory group suspended over T-shirts.* https://www.bbc.co.uk/news/uk-england-cornwall-45735591.   Accessed November 2022.

BBC News (2019). *Inside the Warwick University rape chat scandal.* https://www.bbc.co.uk/news/uk-48366835. Accessed November 2022.

Berlinski, D. J. (1970). *Systems Analysis. Urban Affairs Quarterly, 6*(1), 104–126.

Bond, E., & Phippen, A. (2022a). *Safeguarding adults online: Perspectives on rights to participation.* Policy Press.

Bond, E., & Phippen, A. (2022b). *Higher education online safeguarding self-review tool.* University of Suffolk and Office for National Students https://issuu.com/uniofsuffolk/docs/he-online-safeguarding-self-review-tool-2022-a?fr=sOWU0YjQ5NTg0ODE. Accessed November 2022.

Bronfenbrenner, U. (1979). *The ecology of human development: Experiments by nature and design.* Harvard University Press.

Brook (2019). *Sexual violence and harassment at Universities.* http://legacy.brook.org.uk/data/Brook_DigIN_summary_report2.pdf.   Accessed November 2022.

Brown, M. L., Reed, L. A., & Messing, J. T. (2018). Intimate partner violence and online harassment. In J. Vickery & T. Everbach (Eds.), *Mediating misogyny: Gender, technology, and harassment.* Palgrave Macmillan.

Davidson et al. (2019). *Adult online hate, harassment and abuse: A rapid evidence assessment.* https://assets.publishing.service.gov.uk/government/uploads/system/uploads/attachment_data/file/811450/Adult_Online_Harms_Report_2019.pdf. Accessed November 2022.

Department for Education (2022). *Keeping children safe in education.* https://assets.publishing.service.gov.uk/government/uploads/system/uploads/attachment_data/file/835733/Keeping_children_safe_in_education_2019.pdf. Accessed November 2022.

European Union (2019). *Digital service act ensures safe and accountable online environment.* https://ec.europa.eu/info/strategy/priorities-2019-2024/europe-fit-digital-age/digital-services-act-ensuring-safe-and-accountable-online-environment_en. Accessed November 2022.

Firmin, C. (2020). *Contextual safeguarding and child protection: Rewriting the rules.* Routledge.

Hardt, J., & Rutter, M. (2004). Validity of adult retrospective reports of adverse childhood experiences: Review of the evidence. *Journal of Child Psychology and Psychiatry, 45*(2), 260–273.

Leitão, R. (2021). Technology-Facilitated intimate partner abuse: A qualitative analysis of data from online domestic abuse forums. *Human-Computer Interaction, 36*(3), 203–242.

Messing, J., Bagwell-Gray, M., Brown, M. L., Kappa, A., & Durfee, A. (2020). Intersections of stalking and technology-based abuse: Emerging definitions, conceptualization, and measurement. *Journal of Family Violence, 35*(7), 693–704. https://doi.org/10.1007/s10896-019-00114-.7

Nicolis, G. & Prigogine, Ilya (1989). *Exploring complexity: An introduction*. W H Freeman & Company.

Office for Students (2021). *Statement of expectations on harassment and sexual misconduct.* https://www.officeforstudents.org.uk/media/c1ebedd2-9460-45d0-9cbd-9404122f7378/ofs-statement-of-expectations-on-harassment-and-sexual-misconduct.pdf. Accessed November 2022.

Ofsted (2022). *Inspecting safeguarding in early years, education and skills settings.* https://www.gov.uk/government/publications/inspecting-safeguarding-in-early-years-education-and-skills. Accessed November 2022.

Pardeck, J. T. (1988). An ecological approach for social work practice. *J. Soc. & Soc. Welfare, 15*, 133.

Phippen, A. (2016). *Children's online behaviour and safety: Policy and rights challenges*. Springer.

Phippen, A., & Bond, E. (2020a). *Organisational responses to social media storms: An applied analysis of modern challenges*. Springer Nature.

Phippen. A., & Bond, E. (2020b). *Online harassment and hate crime in HEIs—Report from FOI*. University of Suffolk. https://www.uos.ac.uk/sites/www.uos.ac.uk/files/FOI-Report-Final-Jan-2020-rgb_0.pdf. Accessed November 2022.

Robbins, R., Banks, C., McLaughlin, H., Bellamy, C., & Thackray, D. (2016). Is domestic abuse an adult social work issue? *Social Work Education, 35*(2), 131–143.

Ryan, D. (2001). *Bronfenbrenner's ecological systems theory*. [Online] https://dropoutprevention.org/wpcontent/uploads/2015/07/paquetteryanwebquest_20091110.pdf. Accessed November 2022.

Stroh, D. P. (2015). *Systems thinking for social change: A practical guide to solving complex problems, avoiding unintended consequences, and achieving lasting results*. Chelsea Green Publishing.

Sums Consulting (2022). *Evaluation of the initial impact of the statement of expectations—Final report.* https://www.officeforstudents.org.uk/media/772 fdecd-86d5-4457-8921-4e2969cb634d/evaluation-of-impact-of-statement-of-expectations-final-report.pdf. Accessed November 2022.

Tudge, J. R., Payir, A., Merçon-Vargas, E., Cao, H., Liang, Y., Li, J., & O'Brien, L. (2016). Still misused after all these years? A reevaluation of the uses of Bronfenbrenner's bioecological theory of human development. *Journal of Family Theory & Review, 8*(4), 427–445.

UK Government (2002). *Freedom of Information (Scotland) Act 2002.* http://www.legislation.gov.uk/asp/2002/13/contents. Accessed November 2022.

UK Government (2022). *Online safety bill.* https://bills.parliament.uk/bills/3137. Accessed November 2022.

UK Government (2000). *Freedom of Information Act 2000.* http://www.legislation.gov.uk/ukpga/2000/36/contents. Accessed November 2022.

Universities UK (2022). *Tackling online harassment and promoting online welfare.* https://www.universitiesuk.ac.uk/policy-and-analysis/reports/Pages/tackling-online-harassment.aspx. Accessed November 2022.

Universities UK. (2019). *Changing the culture: Tackling online harassment and promoting online welfare.* https://www.universitiesuk.ac.uk/what-we-do/policy-and-research/publications/tackling-online-harassment-and-promoting. Accessed November 2022.

Wiest-Stevenson, C., & Lee, C. (2016). Trauma-informed schools. *Journal of Evidence-Informed Social Work, 13*(5), 498-503.

Policing Domestic Abuse: A Critical Systems Approach to Surfacing Values, Boundaries, and Assumptions?

Mark Manning

Introduction

The last ten years have seen a proliferation of interest by policymakers in respect of criminal justice responses to DA and Violence Against Women and Girls (VAWG) (College of Policing and National Police Chiefs Council, 2021; Home Office, 2021) and in particular since the newly formed Police and Crime Commissioners became responsible for victims services (Davies, 2022). However, in any attempt to understand how system change occurs within agencies of the criminal justice system (CJS) of England and Wales requires some recognition of the 'workings of the different mechanisms which are established to fulfil such functions for each part of the system' (Garside & Grimshaw, 2022, p. 5). It may be assumed by many that when described as a system, the CJS will have been developed with thought and consideration given to its purpose and with clearly defined boundaries and lines of accountability; if the same

M. Manning (✉)
University of Suffolk, IPSWICH, UK
e-mail: m.manning4@uos.ac.uk

© The Author(s), under exclusive license to Springer Nature Switzerland AG 2024
O. Adisa and E. Bond (eds.), *Tackling Domestic Abuse and Sexual Violence*, Palgrave Studies in Victims and Victimology, https://doi.org/10.1007/978-3-031-58600-2_9

system were to be designed from scratch today, that may be the case. However, in reality, these workings have a history of practice rooted in centuries of custom and common law which has evolved slowly.[1] They are also grounded in the major socio-political and economic changes since industrialisation and the urban growth of the nineteenth century (Garside & Grimshaw, 2022). For policymakers seeking to influence system changes for matters such as DA, there is a problem in that many of the changes required of the CJS and the legal system over the years will have presented as 'wicked problems' which were difficult to resolve and would have frustrated progress.

Termeer et al. (2019) cite ten claims about these wicked problems, among which: they are difficult to define; they have no clear solution, and every wicked problem may be a symptom of another. Examples would include the failure to formally recognise the power and gender imbalances prevalent in society and their impact upon victims of crime, or how, within an adversarial system of justice, to balance the reality of victims' rights against the rights of the accused to a fair trial which are recognised in both custom and statute law (Doak, 2008).

Arguably, in respect of system change and boundary decision-making across the CJS, another claim could be added and that is there is no single component part of the contemporary CJS which has sole responsibility for instituting change, and this is a feature of having a CJS and legal system rooted in custom and common law which by definition has evolved, rather than being transformed. It was previously observed by Rittel and Webber (1973, p. 1), that the search for any scientific (or evidence) bases for confronting problems of social policy (such as DA) was also bound to fail' because of the 'wicked nature' of these problems'. Whilst this statement was made in the context of the USA during the 1970s, it is relevant because of the close cultural connections between the USA and England and Wales, and our shared common law tradition

---

[1] Melville (1901) suggested that our policing system 'rests on foundations designed with the full approval of the people, we know not how many hundreds of years before the Norman conquest and has slowly moulded by the careful hand of experience, developing as a rule along the line of least resistance'. See Melville, W. (1901). A History of Police in England. Kessinger Publishing,

(Roberson & Das, 2016). But this period was also one of systemic avoidance of dealing with DA in a meaningful way which also illustrates how and why broad CJS system changes to DA may have faltered. In part, due to another wicked problem, the juxtaposition of the public expectations for the CJS to treat them fairly and justly, which is in conflict with respective government's political agenda to ensure the CJS is simply fit for purpose and that it runs efficiently (Garside & Grimshaw, 2022). Thus, leaving an implied assumption that justice will naturally follow and as will become clear, perceptions of justice can vary. This is demonstrated in many survey responses from victims of crime (Davis et al., 2013). Added to this perceived 'justice gap' will be differences in the perceived responsibilities of agencies towards each other and the general public. In this sense, Ulrich (2006, p. 1) posits that a critical approach is necessary to understand and resolve these issues as there is no single right way to decide them, and as each of which will be informed by personal interests and surfacing value judgments. How this has reflected in the evolving practices of the CJS and their relationship with systems change will now be explored.

Exploring Systems Change in the Context of the CJS

The criminal justice system in England and Wales, even when viewed as a 'whole', is consistently described as a number of autonomous agencies, each with their own distinctive histories, cultures, and politics (Garside & Grimshaw, 2022, p. 7). Together, they play a part in providing a state response to victims of crime, individuals alleged to have committed a crime and to bring justice to all (Hucklesby & Wahidin, 2013; Joyce, 2017; Joyce & Laverick, 2023; Sanders et al., 2010). It is the autonomous nature of these agencies which creates potential difficulties because far from being an efficient and effective 'whole system' of justice working seamlessly and informed by shared norms and values—the historic nature and evolution of the component parts of this system have been impacted upon by many actors with 'more radical changes occurring at critical junctures where political, social, and cultural atti-tudes became aligned' (Garside & Grimshaw, 2022, p. 7). A good example being, how community concerns over rising crime and anti-social behaviour (ASB) during the 1990s, supported by a theoretical 'Left Realist' call for crime to be taken seriously (Hopkins-Burke, 2019) led New Labour's political response with the introduction of the Crime and Disorder Act 1998 and a raft of policies to deal with youth offending and ASB at a local level. Albeit a critical examination of this system in the sense that Ulrich (2006) suggests, would identify how, over time, the cyclical shifts in political agendas and the value judgements attached to them have had a greater influence on system change rather than the prior judgments of the well-trained professionals and decision-makers working within the component parts of the CJS, and to an extent, any influence exerted upon them by the voting public. This demonstrates how impor-tant it is if in order to effect change, define problems, suggest solutions, and evaluate outcomes—to recognise and understand the prior judge-ments concerning the 'relevant whole system', recognised as boundary judgements (Ulrich, 2006, p. 1).

These boundary judgements are important as they define the bound-aries of the 'whole' reference system and this is a really significant point to reflect upon, because as already illustrated, the CJS is comprised not as a whole, but as a number of autonomous agencies with blurred lines of responsibility and accountability. For this reason, situations will arise which illustrate problems of both boundary decision-making and accountability. For example, in the findings of recent reporting of research concerning Rape and Serious Sexual offences (Stanko, 2022), it is commented that individual police forces cannot create sustainable improvement alone…there are several enabling agencies that could and should support force wide change. The Home Office, National Police Chiefs Council and the Crown Prosecution Service are all mentioned as enablers (Stanko, 2022). In the case of the Crown Prosecution Service, this is one of the key components of the CJS and the one most strongly associated with the police service in the continuance of the criminal justice journey from initial report of a crime to a criminal trial. Whilst this is a boundary which is clearly defined, as are the lines of account-ability, there were tensions raised in the report caused by poor liaison and communication between them (Stanko, 2022, pp. 92–99).

Nonetheless, as a component part of the CJS, it is widely recognised that the police service in England and Wales are the gatekeepers for both victims of crime and offenders, a matter which places them in a unique position (Choi, 2009; Joyce, 2017). However, the office of constable also provides considerable autonomy to them which requires some reflection upon the use of their discretion in order to inform sound judgement (Bottoms & Tankebe, 2012). This reflection is also important to the process of boundary critique (Ulrich, 2006) to ensure that police offi-cers recognise the practical and ethical implications of their decisions within their interactions at the boundaries with other actors—victims of crime, perpetrators, and members of the community who either witness or have a stake in seeing crimes dealt with appropriately (Bowling et al., 2019). However, regardless, of the type of contact or the reason for it, the manner and context of the interaction is likely to shape public percep-tions of the legitimacy of policing through perceptions of whether or not they have been treated fairly and were provided an opportunity to be heard (Bradford et al., 2014).

In terms of systems change at another crucial boundary (Ulrich, 2006) of the CJS—this idea of an investment with other actors within the community as stakeholders presents the police service with a distinctive opportunity to identify, shape, and be reflexive to changes in societal attitudes concerning diverse crime types and potentially, to inform any debates concerning these matters, e.g., DA. However, in practice, this may also be problematic because whilst they can identify emerging crime types very quickly, this is not to say that in terms of boundary setting for CJS systems change (Ulrich, 2006), they are able to, or should be party to influencing political, policy, or legislative changes in the sense that a holistic view of the whole system would require. This is because as high-lighted by Roach (2021), police neutrality in matters of policy is one of their central claims to operational independence and this demonstrates another weakness in the notion of viewing the CJS as a whole system. This is a direct result of the way in which the CJS and the legal system have evolved. For example, whilst the policing of DA has seen a considerable shift in emphasis during the last 20 years towards heightened perceptions of the harm and trauma that it causes (O'Sullivan, 2013; Spalek, 2016); changes within the police service have occurred slowly and often with resistance from within the ranks. This is because their operational independence and their neutrality in matters of policy (Roach, 2021) as a feature of the separation of powers, marks out their own stake in the CJS as an independent component part (Roach, 2021), distinct from other actors such as the Crown Prosecution Service. However, regardless of these claims to independence, there is evidence that over time, policing has evolved sensitivities towards policing DA because the political and cultural landscape has evolved as the next section will illustrate. However, there is a historical context to these developments.

The Changing Political and Cultural Landscape of Policing Domestic Abuse—1970s to 2020s

Beginning with mid-twentieth-century accounts of police responses to DA, there is actually evidence of a systemic avoidance of getting involved in what was regarded as private matters (Brogden, 1991; Choi, 2009; Strickland, 2012; Weinberger, 1995). Until the later 1970s, not only was DA still regarded as a private matter, but there was also a lack of a moral and political will to change this system-wide status quo—leading to the absence of a supportive legislative framework. During this period, despite evidence of a crime being reported to the police, the responsibility to do something about it was left with the victim, usually the wife, and this situation evolved slowly.

However, the same situation prevailed throughout the 1970s and to an extent, the 80s on both sides of the Atlantic (Choi, 2009; Herbert, 1997; Ker Muir, 1977; Sherman, 2018). In many accounts, the perceived dilemma presented to officers responding to DA was how to reconcile any allegations made to them with adequate legal grounds to intervene, and equally commonplace, was the imperative to avoid an arrest at all costs. Generally, this was more for more practical reasons such as the perceived likelihood of the victim withdrawing their complaint (Herbert,

1997; Ker Muir, 1977; Weinberger, 1995). However, as Choi (2009) illustrates, the enduring attitude towards DA by the police service was against a rising tide of public opinion as in 1975, a Parliamentary Select Committee sought to improve the situation in England and Wales. As an illustration of the tensions in systems thinking at the boundaries of CJS decision-making, the police response to questions raised by the committee continued to be resistant, perhaps as a product of retaining their claim to operational independence, but the findings led to the enactment of the Domestic Violence Act 1976 which sought to provide some protection to married women and those cohabiting with a long-term partner. Further, legislation followed with the Housing Act 1977; the Domestic Violence and Magistrates Act 1978, and the Matrimonial Home Act 1983 (Choi, 2009). This legislation was in part brought about to protect victim survivors against the prevailing apathy of the CJS including the police service. This demonstrates how disjointed, and to an extent dysfunctional, the criminal justice system was in terms of both systemic change as well as maintaining social control even when there was a developing political will to do so. Further afield, the United Nations set the Declaration of Basic Principles of Justice for Victims of Crime and Abuse of Power (Spalek, 2016).

In the context of the CJS, an important point to consider here is the extent to which the police service should/could have played at the boundaries of wider system change although Loftus (2009) argues, the police service had become reflexive to changing societal norms. Garside and Grimshaw (2022, p. 7) also report the police were sensitive to pressures from more enlightened communities and pressure groups such as Refuge UK, End Violence against Women and Women's Aid. If so, this is a good example of a 'critical juncture' CJS system change occurring because of an alignment of wider political, social, and cultural changes. However, whatever the causation, and whilst recognising an emerging parallel system of civil remedies; Loftus (2009) argues the trend in policing had been towards iterative and increased levels of support, with Spalek (2016) highlighting how the CJS had become more willing to provide legal remedies through the criminal courts. With court-related services provided to reduce the fear of the experience.

Another important movement to achieve this response was the shift towards debating DA and other abuses of power as a social justice issue in recognition that not all jurisdictions would invoke criminal legislation for these harms, but which still required societal recognition and more importantly, support (Spalek, 2016). Perhaps some assumptions were made concerning surfacing societal values supportive of a social justice approach, but the idea of utilising this lens to create wider systemic change was also informed by a new theoretically informed victimology movement (Spalek, 2016)—driven by emerging socio-political debates which seemed to suggest it gained public support and to an extent, a political voice informed by the pressure groups. This demonstrates that for a CJS to be effective, it should be axiomatic that democratic and political control are essential ingredients for improving responses to DA, to promote broad system change, and to influence policy supportive of the legitimate non-prosecutorial support services identified as missing in earlier responses to DA. Also raised as issues by an evolution of thought which would later reflect an emphasis upon human rights and sensitivity to high harm and vulnerability (Doak, 2008; Gelsthorpe, 2013).

Illustrating the complexities of boundary decision-making for the component parts of the CJS in terms of system change (Ulrich, 2006), the move towards identifying DA as a social justice issue was also in recognition of the fact that legislators would need to provide a clear and more effective legal remedy before the CJS and the police service as a component part, could provide a satisfactory response to victims of DA. However, another perspective offered by Termeer and Biesbroek (2019) is that these wicked problems are complex, and even when there is a desire to act, politicians often lack the capacity or political will to do so, directly through the CJS. However, in reality, the rise of victimology as a social movement provided a far more insightful way of thinking about systems change for victims and victimhood, and a reflection upon its influence towards a heightened awareness of risk and harm is also worthy of reflection as an incremental step in a broader system change.

The Rise of the Victim Status

According to Maitra et al. (2023) the recent ascendance of the #MeToo movement emanating from the United States (US), and the murders of Sabina Nessa, Sarah Everard, Nicole Smallman, and Bibaa Henry in the UK, has heightened a contemporary public debate about gendered violence and the right to feel safe in public in the twenty-first century. However, it has taken a long whilst for women and girls to be recognised as such as these accounts have a history in which the rise of victim status can be grounded. The contested nature or status of the victim in society and in the criminal courts was highlighted among others by Christie (1977, 1986) who illustrated both the complexities of being a victim of crime in need of support, as well as his notion of the 'ideal victim' most likely to gain support. In doing so, he raised awareness of the plight of victim status in the CJS. Although, as Kearon and Godfrey (2007) indicate, the 'Ideal victims' characterised by Christie (1986) were the least likely group to be victimised with the most likely being, as for offenders—young, working class, and male.

However, towards the end of the twentieth century, practical steps had already been taken across the world by surveying populations to explore the size and scale of crime victimisation (Spalek, 2016). This interest emerged from much wider debates concerning increasing levels of crime, the resultant 'fear of crime', and its social consequences (Walklate, 2007). Garland (2002) emphasised the state response to this issue to be increased surveillance and a heightened awareness towards crime control; whilst Beck (1992, p. 19) identified the emergence of a systematic social production of risk in what he described as 'the new paradigm of risk society'. This evolution of thought led politicians and CJS policymakers to an increasingly complex policy shift towards risk and risk assessment (Gelsthorpe, 2013). However, this policy shift also coincided with a 'new managerialist' reorientation of the relationship between public services and citizens towards a characterisation of service providers and consumers, in a quest for the increased efficiencies enjoyed by the private sector (Doak, 2008). Whilst this characterisation created new layers of complexity in terms of boundary decision-making such as managing risk and performance measurement, it produced some advantages such as a willingness to develop victim-centred policies (Doak, 2008). However, regardless of this origin, the status of victims in the courts continued to remain a contested space with the accused enjoying all the rights in a due process and adversarial system of justice (Matravers, 2010).

The Rise of New Labour and the Evolution of Policy and Practice

This initial history is important as it illustrates how, in respect of victims of DA, system change has been iterative and slow, and as has also been illustrated, there are several contested theoretical lenses through which to explain it. In terms of systems thinking to improve the CJS response to DA, the identification of a left realist theoretical 'square of crime' was influential for emphasising the complex relationship between the public, the criminal justice system, the offender, and the victim of crime as being interlinked in the sense that when there is an action from one, it creates a reaction from another which requires a balance of intervention (Burke, 2019). For example, to deliver a successful intervention for domestic abuse requires, at least, for victims to feel confident to report these crimes to the police for investigation and to seek help from support services. This raises awareness and informs public opinion in order to garner support. The public may, in turn, influence a response from policymakers and the CJS to do something positive about it. It can be seen that there are several layers for policy intervention within this theoretical approach, but the police form only part of that approach and this presents a complex area for system change. It was the rise of New Labour ideology partly influenced by Young and Lea, which led to such an evolution of policy and practice (Joyce, 2017). It also created a moral imperative to do so, because they highlighted how victims were being ignored by politicians and legislators alike and there was a body of research to support that fact.

In a summary to Parliament of 'New Labour' policy towards domestic abuse from 1999 to 2010 Strickland, (2012, p. 2) reaffirms the historical context already discussed throughout this chapter but emphasises that during the 1980s, there was a body of developing research which demonstrated that 'few perpetrators of domestic abuse were prosecuted or even arrested'. This research would inform a more progressive system change in response to DA. Having assumed responsibility for change through developing policy, the Home Office published Living without Fear—An Integrated Approach to Tackling Violence against Women (1999) and commissioned a series of research papers towards an evidence informed 'What Works' agenda to reduce this violence (Strickland, 2012).

Within the subsequent white paper titled 'Justice for All' an agenda was set for consultation which would lead to policy and 'legislative changes involving risk management, use of both criminal and civil law remedies, policing, accommodation, and perpetrator programmes' (Strickland, 2012, p. 3). This led to the enactment of the Domestic Violence Crime and Victims Act 2004 making common assault an arrestable offence (Strickland, 2012). This was an important new power for police officers to utilise when attending reports of DA where only minor injuries were sustained as it provided the power to take positive action.[2] Other changes included—cohabiting and same-sex couples were provided access to non-molestation orders punishable on indictment—previously only available to heterosexual partners and finally, allowing the courts to impose restraining orders under the Protection of Harassment Act 1997 (Strickland, 2012). On the face of it, this raft of changes was a move in the right direction towards systemic changes in the response to DA.

Further, in 2004, as part of the developing policy shift, the Code of Practice for Victims of Crime was published which informed victims of what they could expect from the CJS and how to hold the system to account (Spalek, 2016). The code also stipulated what CJS agencies—the police, Probation Service, Crown Prosecution Service, and Courts Service must do for victims. However, whilst this code was progressive in terms of system change, it did not go as far as expressing these service provisions specifically as rights even when they were expressed

---

[2] . This power was repealed by the Serious Organised and Police Act 2005 which extended powers of arrest for all offences where arrest conditions were met Strickland (2012),

more clearly in the revised Code of Practice 2013—published by the Ministry of Justice (Spalek, 2016). The latest iteration of the victims code (2020) does express these rights more formally, but in reality, their impact remains largely peripheral to legal processes.

In summary, whilst Joyce (2017) does not restrict his support of Left Realist ideology to domestic abuse, he argues in general support of New Labour and the matters discussed here, and how through their mantra 'Tough on Crime, Tough on Causes of Crime' they seemed to recognise the causal factors and necessary responses required by policy to support the balance of interventions proposed by Young and Lea. In the context of system change, it was a catalyst for progressive change, albeit structural, but involving the police as only part of that change.

Victims and Human Rights

This final section will explore claims that reconceiving victims' rights as human rights (Doak, 2008) has led to an evolution of police and multi-agency CJS practices. In terms of system change, this seemed to suggest that an end was in sight along the victim journey. Albeit as observed Spalek (2016) it is argued that these rights did not go as far as delivering equal rights because of the contested place of the victim within the CJS.

Doak, (2008, p. 1) went as far as to suggest that 'the phenomenon of victims' rights had been catapulted to the forefront of policymaking on both domestic and international platforms'. Although, in the context of the legal system of England and Wales, Matravers (2010) emphasised the importance of also recognising the relative constitutional place of victims and the State, and civil society in the CJS. An element of which requires a deeper understanding of the position of the State, its relation to morality and community, together with an informed debate concerning 'who owns crimes'—the state or the parties involved? (Matravers, 2010, pp.1–4). This is a complex debate which can only explored with a light touch here, but it will become clear that the evolution of rights alone, did not provide the broad system change or legal remedy that many would have wished for. It is clearly recognised that a greater awareness of the risk and harm experienced by victims of crime gave rise to a better understanding of victim status and the pain and suffering associated with it (Beck, 1992; Gelsthorpe, 2013; Spalek, 2016; Walklate, 2007). Matravers (2010) observes that much has also been done to improve the experience of victims through the CJS process and this is to be welcomed. Policy development supporting victims through CJS processes has also been improved (College of Policing and National Police Chiefs Council, 2021; Home Office, 2021). That said, the state response by the provision of policy and legislative changes was not an end in themselves. Albeit the advent of human rights implied that rights created obligations upon the state which may have led to cementing the status of victims in a more solid foundation.

Doak (2008, p. 19) highlights, one of the core arguments is 'that the prospect of realising rights for victims is intimately connected with ideas about the proper role they ought to play in criminal justice'. This implies the provision of rights-based moral obligations as a normative condition. However, as Doak (2008) also illustrates, whilst this position is often alluded to in academic discourse and in non-legal contexts, it causes confusion as to the precise role of rights in a CJS context. Put simply, the contentious question is how to balance the reality of victims' rights against the rights of the accused to a fair trial as offered by the Human Rights Act 1998—article 6, within an adversarial system of justice.

Summary and Conclusion

In summary, the state has the 'legitimate claim on the case as the only institution with the resources to represent everyone' (Matravers, 2010, p. 7). As such, article 6 exists to maintain the 'offenders' right to a fair trial in which the victim is replaced by the state as the legitimate prosecuting authority. The victim then appears as a witness to deliver oral testimony in court and is bound by the rules of evidence (Doak, 2008). As Doak (2008) further explains, even with the provision of human rights and standards, some of which are legally binding, they are unlikely to improve the position of the victims in domestic CJ systems and they will continue to be denied rights as a matter of fact or by right, as there is no coherent statement of legal rights for victims within the CJS in

England and Wales. Arguably, the most recent publication of the Code of Practice for Victims of Crime in England and Wales (2020) has done nothing to advance the position previously articulated by Doak (2008) and Matravers (2010). The New code does refer to what were previously referred to as service provisions as 'rights' and they are intended to keep the victim informed and to improve their experience through the CJS process. However, they remain largely peripheral to the investigation and trial process. In terms of system change for DA within the CJS and by the police as a component part, questions remain concerning how a system-wide CJS could or should perform in relation to supporting victim survivors. Critically, it can be seen that even when there is political will to change policy to effect change - the complexity of the CJS as a whole reference system and in particular, the legal context, leaves some hurdles to overcome, despite travelling so far.

Implications for Policy

This chapter has illustrated that there remains a tendency to think of policy development in terms of institutional responsibilities without considering the implications for policy and practice. Future developments concerning DA should take account of how the CJS as a whole reference system can be improved by policymakers, to improve the journey of the victim survivor through the CJS and the legal system.

However, bearing in mind the evolution of thought and support for victims of crime over the last decade, the most important area for continued debate is how to resolve the wicked problem of the tension between the defendant's right to a fair trial taking priority over the rights of victims. This is a complex and multi-faceted debate which should involve communities, victims interest groups, policymakers, the component parts of the CJS, the legal system, and legislators. This could lead to the provision of a more coherent statement of legal rights for victims within the CJS in England and Wales.

References

Beck, U. (1992). *Risk society: Towards a new modernity*. Sage.

Bottoms, A., & Tankebe, J. (2012). Beyond procedural justice: A dialogic approach to legitimacy in criminal justice. *The Journal of Criminal Law & Criminology, 102*(1), 119–170. Retrieved from https://www.jstor.org/stable/23145787

Bowling, B., Reiner, R., & Sheptycki, J. W. E. (2019). *The politics of the police* (5th ed.). Oxford University Press.

Bradford, B., Murphy, K., & Jackson, J. (2014). OFFICERS AS MIRRORS: Policing, procedural justice and the (re)production of social identity. *British Journal of Criminology, 54*(4), 527–550. https://doi.org/10.1093/bjc/azu021

Brogden, M. (1991). *On the Mersey beat policing Liverpool between the wars*. Oxford University Press.

Burke, R. H. (2019). *An introduction to criminological theory* (5th ed.). Routledge.

Choi, K. (2009). Tackling domestic violence in UK: Persistent problems. *International Area Review, 12*(1), 17–43. https://doi.org/10.1177/223386590901200103

Christie, N. (1977). Conflicts as property. *The British Journal of Criminology, 17*(1), 1–15.

Christie, N. (1986). The ideal victim. In E. A. Fattah (Ed.), *From crime policy to victim policy: Reorienting the justice system* (pp. 17–30). Houndmills.

Code of practice for victims of crime in England and Wales (2020). Ministry of Justice.

College of Policing and National Police Chiefs Council (2021). Policing violence against women and girls. National Framework for delivery: Year 1. College of Policing. Available online @ Policing violence against women and girls - National framework for delivery: Year 1 (npcc.police.uk).

Davies, P. (2022). How far has multi-agency policing travelled in 30 years? Reflecting on progress in the context of 'policing' domestic abuse in England and Wales. *Crime Prevention and Community Safety, 24*, 311–327.

Davis, R., Lurigio, A., & Herman, S. (2013). *Victims of Crime* (4th ed.). Sage Publications

Doak, J. (2008). *Victims' rights, human rights and criminal justice* (1st ed.). Bloomsbury Publishing (UK). https://doi.org/10.5040/9781472564351

Garland, D. G. (2002). *The culture of control: Crime and social order in contemporary society*. Oxford University Press.

Garside, R., & Grimshaw, R. (2022). *Criminal justice systems in the UK governance, inspection, complaints, and accountability.* Centre for Crime and Justice Studies.

Gelsthorpe, L. (2013). *Criminal justice: The policy landscape.* Oxford University Press. https://doi.org/10.1093/he/9780199694969.003.0001

Herbert, S. K. (1997). *Policing space* (NED - New edition ed.). Minneapolis [u.a.]: Univ. of Minnesota Press. https://doi.org/10.5749/j.ctttsj2f

Home Office (2021). Tackling violence against women and girls. HM Government. Available online @ Tackling violence against women and girls (publishing.service.gov.uk).

Hopkins-Burke, R. (2019). *An introduction to criminological theory* (5th ed.). Routledge.

Hucklesby & Wahidin. (2013). *Criminal justice* (2nd ed.). Oxford University Press

Joyce, P. & Laverick, W. (2023). *Criminal justice* (4th ed.). Routledge.

Joyce, P. (2017). *Criminal justice* (3rd ed.). Routledge.

Kearon, T., & Godfrey, B. S. (2007). Setting the scene: A question of history. In S. Walklate (Ed.), *Handbook of victims and victimology* (pp. 17–35) Willan. https://doi.org/10.4324/9780203118207-7

Ker Muir, W. (1977). *Police street corner politicians.* The University of Chicago Press.

Loftus, B. (2009). *Police culture in a changing world.* Oxford University Press.

Maitra, D., Allen, K., Hermolle, M., & Adisa, O. (2023). *Sexual harassment in public spacesCommunicating harms and challenging perpetration.*

Matravers, M. (2010). The victim, the state and civil society. In A. Bottoms, & J. V. & Roberts (Eds.), *Hearing the victim adversarial justice, crime victims and the state* (pp. 1–16)

O'Sullivan, C. S. (2013). Sexual violence victimisation of women, men, youth and children. In R. C. Davis, A. J. Lurigio, & S. Herman (Eds.), *Victims of crime* (pp. 3–28). Sage.

Roach, K. (2021). Balancing police independence and political responsibility for the police: Some recent developments in Australia, Canada, and the UK. *Policing : A Journal of Policy and Practice, 15*(1), 133–149. https://doi.org/10.1093/police/pay055

Rittel, H., & Webber, M. (1973). Dilemmas in a general theory of planning. *Journal of Policy Sciences, 4*(2). Elsevier Scientific Publishing Company

Roberson, C., & Das, D. (2016). *Comparative legal models of criminal justice.* CRC Press.

Sanders, A., Young, R., & Burton M. (2010). *Criminal justice* (4th ed.). Oxford University Press.

Sherman, L. W. (2018). Policing domestic violence 1967–2017. *Criminology and Public Policy, 17*(2), 453–465. https://doi.org/10.1111/1745-9133.12365

Spalek, B. (2016). *Crime victims* (2nd ed.). Bloomsbury Publishing Plc. https://ebookcentral.proquest.com/lib/[SITE_ID]/detail.action?docID=6234362

Stanko, B. (2022). Operation Soteria Bluestone Year 1 Report 2021–2022. Home Office. Available online @ Operation Soteria Year One Report—GOV.UK. www.gov.uk

Strickland, P. (2012). *Labour policy on domestic violence—1999–2010 SN/HA/3989*. House of Commons Library.

Termeer, C., Dewulf, A., & Biesbroek, R. (2019). A critical as assessment of the wicked problem concept: Relevance and usefulness for policy science and practice. *Policy and Society, 2*(38), 167–179. https://doi.org/10.1080/14494035.2019.1617971

Ulrich, W. (2005). *A brief introduction to critical systems heuristics (CSH)*. Ecosensus Publications.

Walklate, S. (2007). *Handbook of victims and victimology*. Willan. https://doi.org/10.4324/9780203118207

Weinberger, B. (1995). *The best police in the world*. Scolar Press.

Index

© The Editor(s) (if applicable) and The Author(s), under exclusive
license to Springer Nature Switzerland AG 2024
O. Adisa and E. Bond (eds.), *Tackling Domestic Abuse and Sexual Violence*, Palgrave
Studies in Victims and Victimology, https://doi.org/10.1007/978-3-031-58600-2

Printed by Printforce, United Kingdom